ANTIQUE JEWELRY:
A Practical & Passionate Guide

A Practical & Passionate Guide

by Rose Leiman Goldemberg

Photographs by Edward R. Height, Jr.
Line drawings based on original
sketches by Minda Novek and Lee Schiller

AN AUTHORS GUILD BACKINPRINT.COM EDITION

Antique Jewelry:
A Practical & Passionate Guide

All Rights Reserved © 1976, 2000 by Rose Leiman Goldemberg

No part of this book may be reproduced or transmitted in any form
or by any means, graphic, electronic, or mechanical, including photocopying,
recording, taping, or by any information storage or retrieval system,
without the permission in writing from the publisher.

AN AUTHORS GUILD BACKINPRINT.COM EDITION

Published by iUniverse.com, Inc.

For information address:
iUniverse.com, Inc.
620 North 48th Street, Suite 201
Lincoln, NE 68504-3467
www.iuniverse.com

Originally published by Crown Publishers

Designed by Laurie Zuckerman

ISBN: 0-595-08898-8

Printed in the United States of America

To my husband, Bob,
and to my children, Lee and Lisa,
who have shared with me the
pleasures of "the portable art"

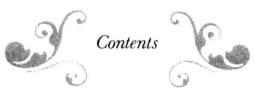

Contents

Acknowledgments

There is no way of adequately thanking all the people—friends, dealers, scholars, associates—whose encouragement and generous sharing of knowledge helped make this book a reality.

I would like to single out, however, a few of the many for a warm and special expression of gratitude. To the many museum curators—most especially Mrs. Claire LeCorbeiller of the Metropolitan Museum of Art, Mr. Philip Curtis of the Newark Museum, Mrs. Susan McTigue of the Museum of the City of New York, Mr. John Noble of the Museum of the City of New York, and Mrs. Mary Black of the New-York Historical Society—who made their fine collections of old jewelry available for study and discussion, my grateful thanks.

I want also to thank Mr. Robert Arnold, Senior Conservator at the Metropolitan Museum of Art, and Mrs. Dora Jane Jansen, a scholar and author of great learning in this and other fields, who unstintingly gave of their information and enthusiasm.

In the years I have loved old jewelry I have been more than fortunate in counting among my friends many dealers who have shared my passion and far outstripped me in knowledge. I owe a great deal to all of them, and particularly to Mrs. Enid Goldman of The Gold Man, Mrs. Regina Sinofsky, Mrs. Nadia Shepard of Old Mine Road Antiques, and Mrs. Patricia Goldstein of Small and Perfect, whose standards, taste, and experience are extraordinary.

Finally, my gratitude to Mrs. Georgette Henry, whose zeal and expertise in typing this manuscript were a "good right hand" to me—and a left one, too!

ROSE LEIMAN GOLDEMBERG
January 31, 1976

 *Introduction*

How does one begin to write about a hobby that is also a passion—a pastime that can also be a livelihood—an investment that also informs and enriches one's human understanding?

A decade ago, I really didn't know that antique jewelry existed. When my mother died, she left a few modest pieces of family jewelry—a ring my grandmother had worn, a ring of my grandfather's, a small stickpin, her own well-loved cameos and bar pins. And from owning these, my own collection—and passion—has grown. For my grandmother's ring appeared in a picture of her as a young bride. I remembered my grandfather's ring on his finger. And my mother's jewelry reminded me of rich family occasions when she had worn it with pleasure and pride. In little, these few pieces reflected the truth about *all* antique jewelry—they were intensely personal, beloved, human, and beautiful.

People wear jewelry only if they *want* to; it reflects taste, the times, the individual. The love of jewelry goes back literally to the birth of what we understand as "civilization." For pleasure, for magic, for enhancement of beauty, for investment—human creatures have loved jewelry as long as they have been human. And what they have loved—and worn—tells us about them: who they were, the shape of their clothes and their bodies, the materials they treasured, the symbols they lived by, and what they considered valuable and beautiful.

Through collecting and wearing old jewelry—and preserving it and passing it on in good condition—you are sharing in human history. You are investing in art you can wear. You are lovingly preserving a part of the past for the future. Learning to know the jewelry feeds your knowledge of history, of costume, of art, and of the human heart. And if you travel, the pleasure of exploring a new town's treasures is hard to improve on.

But these are all after-the-fact rationalizations. The real reason for collecting old jewelry is because you *love* it—because it "speaks" to you. And if it does, and you are admiring it, or have already begun to buy, you need more than your own taste (important as that is) to guide you in looking, choosing, evaluating, and buying pieces that are really *right* and that will repay your love and your initial investment with years of pleasurable wear *and* enhanced value.

This book is written as a down-to-earth, concise, specific guide for the American collector. It deals with the jewelry that is available and worth buying, tells how to find it, identify it, judge it, and—providing that you *do* buy it—wear it, take care of it, and preserve it for future pleasure.

It is the book I wish I had had when I started collecting.

In this country it is not easy for the collector—or even the dealer, for that matter—to learn about antique jewelry. Museums are, on the whole, disinterested in jewelry as an art or as a tool to understand the past. They exhibit *ancient* jewelry—but the jewelry of our grandmothers and grandfathers, or even *their* grandparents, does not appeal to American curators. America is still a Puritan country after all, unwilling to admit that what is "frivolous" can also be important and meaningful. It is not this way in Europe, where huge halls of great museums are devoted to jewelry, and fine specimens are eagerly sought after. Perhaps the burgeoning interest in costume in America will eventually grow to envelop jewelry; after all, jewelry is the hors d'oeuvre of costume. But at this writing, most museums, though they have been bequeathed jewelry from time to time, rarely exhibit it, have little interest in it, and usually keep it locked securely away in dark vaults, far from the admiring eyes of those of us who would love to study and enjoy it.

Most of the books in print about jewelry are of little help to the beginning American collector. The pieces they illustrate are magnificent royal heirlooms, far beyond the reach of the average buyer. And the information they share is primarily historical—interesting and important, yes, but about as useful to the modest collector as a book on decorating Windsor Castle would be to a new young bride.

The jewelry that is for sale is often mislabeled, spoiled, poorly handled, misunderstood. Many dealers, especially those who are not specialists in jewelry, know almost nothing about it, and pass on misinformation that grows, changes, and is exaggerated with every sale; by the time it gets to you, what the dealer tells you (which she may firmly believe is what was told to her) bears as much resemblance to the truth as the Legend of Sleepy Hollow. Indeed, much fiction is told about jewelry, and part of your task as a lover and buyer is to learn to separate fact from fiction, and truly recognize and understand what you are buying, what it is worth, and how to take care of it properly.

On the other hand, most of the real, specific knowledge about old jewelry in this country lies with dealers—primarily dealers who work exclusively with jewelry. I, myself, owe a huge debt to the dealer/friends who have generously shared their knowledge and their passion for the "portable art" with me.

But if one has no dealer/friend with learning, if there is no museum collection to study, no course to take (and I have never seen a single course offered in antique jewelry in this country), how is the fledgling collector to learn?

I hope this book will be a beginning.

Then, with the book in hand, you must learn from your jewelry itself and from all the pieces that you are privileged to study. It can be a love affair that will last a lifetime!

One word of definition: since the purpose of this book is to inform you about jewelry *you can buy,* there is no point in describing pieces that realistically you can expect only to see pictured in books or (if you are lucky) displayed in museums. For all practical purposes, an American collector can rarely buy jewelry earlier than nineteenth century, and most of what you see will date from 1860 or later. On the other hand, much of the "antique" jewelry that is being shown and bought dates from much later, primarily from the turn of the century through the Art Deco period of the 1920s and 1930s. This "old" jewelry is nevertheless much beloved and well worth buying and wearing. It is different in spirit and design from modern jewelry, reflects a value system and sense of beauty that is specific to its own time and different from ours, and is more abundant, generally in better condition, and more readily buyable than pieces that date back to an earlier time. For the purposes of this book, then, let us address ourselves primarily to jewelry made and worn from 1800 to the 1920s, or roughly from the American Revolution to the Great Stock Market crash of 1929.

For clarity, I will use the terms most dealers use—"Victorian" for jewelry made and worn during the reign of England's Queen Victoria (1837–1901), "Georgian" for pre-Victorian jewelry worn during the reign of the first four English Georges, and "Edwardian" for pieces made while Edward VII reigned in England, 1901–10. In fact, since America, as a young and struggling country, produced little jewelry, much of the fine old jewelry available to us here is either English or French.

Further, as American collectors of modest means, you will probably not be buying "primary" jewelry—magnificent diamond dog collars and ropes of pearls—or if you are, you will need more than the knowledge one book can impart. So this guide will concentrate on the more modest "secondary" jewelry, often made as day (rather than formal evening) jewelry: pieces that sell now for as little as five dollars or as much, perhaps, as a thousand, but which, in workmanship, adornment, beauty, and investment potential are truly worth owning and which faithfully speak to us of the unique spirit of their times.

Chapter One

The Whys and Hows of Dealing with Dealers

What is the fascination of antique jewelry, anyhow? Why do women—and men—cluster around the jewelry dealers at antique shows, leaning eagerly over the counters to get a closer look at what sometimes is very meager fare? Why do mothers hand down to their daughters "grandma's wedding ring," or pass on to their sons' sons a grandfather's gold watch? Of course there is a beauty in preserving one's own family heirlooms, but the charm of old jewelry far outshines that personal goal. It speaks of a time gone; it has *survived* in a disrespectful world where so much is lost; it comes from an age when workmanship and fine craft were taken seriously; it is often beautiful in a mellow and mature way that "modern design" does not aspire to; and it has been proven, through centuries of collecting, to be an investment unparalleled in these times of insecure "securities." In centuries past, and indeed still today, jewelry is the most "portable" wealth—it is an international "currency," an investment that is also an enormous pleasure, an heirloom that is also contemporary in its timeless beauty. I have often said that if I came into a windfall, I would not buy stock or take a trip; I'd find the finest piece of Georgian gold jewelry I could afford and buy it, wear it, or vault it—but my guess is that in

1

twenty years my investment would have grown as greatly as any other I could have made, and would have given me much more pleasure.

Of course modern jewelry can be beautiful and valuable too. But old jewelry has an additional charm; it is, for the most part, unique. In your hunting you may find *similar* pieces, pieces that are better or lesser examples of a "style," but seldom—very seldom—will you find *two pieces exactly alike.* (If you do, watch out! But more of this later.) Though there is certainly plenty of "mass-produced" old jewelry on the market, so much has been lost that even once-commonplace pieces may now be rare. Materials that were once worn like costume jewelry—tortoise, gutta-percha, bog oak, gunmetal, even sterling silver—are now, with their age upon them, respected for the glimpse they give us of other times, their rarity, and (often) their very real beauty. Because of this *uniqueness,* the finding and buying of old jewelry takes on a very *personal* quality; to seek out and find the very best piece of its kind and buy it—and to own it—gives a special thrill that cannot be compared with the tamer pleasures of ordering a piece (no matter how beautiful) out of a catalog, or buying it from a jeweler's showcase.

Most of us, when we begin to collect, have modest means and even less assurance. We are not buying diamond tiaras; we are hanging shyly around dealers' counters hungering for an old ring, perhaps, or a cameo, or a Scotch agate pin, or a pair of coral earrings. And we are wondering—and unsure as to how to find out—is it real? Is it reasonably priced? Is it old? Is it good of its kind? Will it stand up to reasonable wear or fall apart in a disappointingly short time? Can the dealer be trusted?

As we get more sophisticated, some of these questions seem to answer themselves, but others stay with us, as insistent as ever. It is one of the purposes of this book to answer those questions, *specifically* for beginning and more sophisticated collectors alike. The more educated the buyer, the more educated the dealer must become—and that advances the "state of the art." The more educated *you* become, the better "appreciator" you will be—the more able to recognize a truly "super" piece, a truly "good buy," or, conversely, a fake, a worthless "put-together" piece, or an honest—but *new*—"reproduction."

There is more to antique jewelry than the buying and owning of it, too. Old pieces, like old people, tend to be fragile, to have "ills" that must be detected, and corrected, if you are to pass them on as beautiful as you found them. Ivory tends to warp and split, tortoise to get dull or crack, pearls to be attacked by acids, coral to chip and fall to pieces, gold to wear, silver to tarnish, hair to decay. And yet, with a little proper care, each of them can be preserved or even brought back to full beauty. With a little—only a little—misuse, they can be ruined forever.

Many old pieces were not designed to be worn the same way as we wear our jewelry now. The fabrics they sat on were different from those we favor, styles were different, customs were not the same. To put on a pair of old earrings correctly may mean the difference between wearing them for years or breaking them down so that they have to be rebuilt or may even be lost. Pins without safety catches (an invention of the second decade of the twentieth century) were seldom lost by their owners but are often lost by us *because we don't know how to attach them properly.*

This book, therefore, will deal not only with collecting and buying old jewelry, but with wearing it and taking care of it, as well. May the jewelry live forever—and may you pass it on in the same or better condition than it was passed to you!

In your collecting you will be spending a lot of time looking at pieces and talking to dealers. There is an art to this, too, as any serious collector of *anything* knows. It is worthwhile, I think, to spend a little time discussing this technique—for it is a kind of art.

First of all, to get maximum help and information from a dealer, you must assume that he or she* is a human being like you and as much interested in old jewelry as you are. This seems banal, but think about it. Often one's attitude toward a dealer is an adversary attitude: she has what I want, will try to sell it too high, will conceal its faults from me, considers me a fool for not knowing enough or for loving too foolishly to hold out for a better price. Admittedly, all this may be true! But, practically speaking, assuming it is true will do you harm. More likely, the dealer is an ordinary enough human being—in business for profit, yes, but at least as honorable as you are, with some knowledge (sometimes awesome knowledge, sometimes abysmally little) and a reasonable willingness to share it. In my own experience, a dealer has almost never lied to me when asked straight-on questions. Therefore I make it a point to ask them—including what is sometimes the "key question": Is that your best price? *or* Do you have any give on the price? *or* Can you do a little better? Many dealers expect this—and have inflated their price a bit to give you the pleasure of slipping it down. Others have firm prices and will tell you so. But if your manner is businesslike and pleasant, theirs will be too. "Is this your best price?" is as legitimate a question as "Is it your policy to give cash

---

*The majority of antique jewelry dealers are women—though there are plenty of men in the field, too. For the purposes of this book, therefore, I will refer to the dealer as *she*

refunds or credit slips?" is in a dress shop, and it will be accepted that way if you ask it that way. What a dealer does react to—and sometimes dramatically!—is scoffing, putting down the merchandise, implying that it is no good and therefore not worth what is being asked, or making a ridiculously low counteroffer. I have seen customers insist that an 18K mark was a fake, that a gold piece was not gold (without even having examined it under a loupe), and then offer a price a tenth of the marked value of a piece. The dealer in this case was a good deal more patient than I would have been. But she refused to go on with the sale—and humanly speaking, she was absolutely right! This kind of behavior—which usually stems from insecurity and lack of knowledge—is grossly impolite and will meet with no luck from any legitimate dealer.

What should your behavior be, then? Of course there's no single answer to this question, but I will tell you what has stood me in good stead for many (more than I should admit!) purchases. My etiquette for "dealing with dealers" is this:

1. First, wait patiently until the dealer can give her whole attention to you. Use your time to examine the pieces for sale so that when you are waited on you can ask specifically and without wasting time for those you want to see more closely.

2. When your turn comes, point out the pieces you want to see. Do *not* ask the price at this point. If the dealer volunteers it (and she may if the piece is expensive because she does not want to waste time with anyone not interested in that price class), accept the information, but don't pursue it. *Never discuss price or bargain for any piece you have no real interest in buying.* This is both good manners and good sense.

3. Examine the pieces you ask to see—carefully, respectfully, and thoroughly. Ask all the questions you have about them, and listen to the answers. (See chapters four and five for more about the questions.) Listen, as well, to the dealer's style. If she is pushing a sale, doing more to convince you than merely exhibiting a personal enthusiasm for the piece, a little red flag should go up in your mind: *Why?* Often dealers will not know the answers to your questions. "I don't know" is a good, honest answer (and nearly always a truthful one). I have learned not to trade information with most dealers (although I sometimes know things they do not—and so will you) unless they really demonstrate a love and respect for the jewelry they sell. Most dealers have that love; many do not, and do not want to be informed either. If this latter is true, don't waste your time and breath trying to explain why a necklace marked "amber" is plastic or a chain marked "Georgian" *isn't*. But if the dealer is genuinely interested and enthusiastic, she will be eager to learn and

to share information—and perhaps more pleased to sell a treasure to someone who appreciates it than to someone who does not.

4. If you are truly interested in buying the piece at the right price, *ask the price.* All pieces should be marked, but often they are not—or they are marked in code, which gives the dealer a chance to inch the price up or down according to her assessment of you. As with everything else, there is a human factor in dealing with dealers. If you are fair, reasonable, and polite with them, they are more likely to treat you in the same way. *Never, never* talk a piece down in order to force the price down. It is the mark of an insecure and crude buyer. There are better ways of achieving the same result (buying the piece at the best price the dealer will sell it for) and coming away with your dignity—and the dealer's—intact.

There is nothing wrong with asking if there is any "give" on the price. Most dealers expect a bit of jockeying and are prepared for it. If your dealer is not, she will let you know. But this kind of discussion should never take place unless you are prepared to buy. The dealer, remember, has a certain financial investment in the piece, and is entitled to a fair profit; you know what you can afford to spend. Between these two sums, a price should be set that leaves both of you feeling good—and wanting to do business with each other again.

5. If you decide not to buy, do so in a way that leaves the door open for you to come and look again, or even to buy this piece should your feelings (or the dealer's price) change. I wish I had a fine hair watch chain for all the times I have said, "No thank you. I can't manage that," and then gone looking for days, maybe even years, for another piece like the one I did *not* buy. My rule is this: if you love it and can afford it, buy it, providing it meets all the requirements in chapters four and five. But "love" means *really* love. The test is this: go away for ten minutes, have a cup of coffee, and think about coming back to the dealer and finding that someone else has bought your piece. If you feel, "Well, it wasn't for me; so be it," don't buy. But if your stomach knots up with the loss, and you want to jump up, leave your coffee, and run back before somebody else steals your treasure, a purchase is definitely indicated.

Price, after all, is relative. Many dealers will tell you—and it is often true—that they set their price according to what they paid for a piece. If they overpaid, you will too. If they got a bargain, they may pass a bargain on. If they have had a piece for a long time and would like to move it so that they can buy something else, you may get a real "buy" on it. The dealer, after all, can stay in business only by turning stock over so that money is released to buy new stock. Pieces that languish in the display case really cost a dealer money. So most dealers want to sell, unless they have a piece of such excellence that they would cheerfully keep it for themselves or put it in the vault to accrue in value if it doesn't appeal to buyers in a reasonable time.

If you agree on a price with a dealer, and then for some reason you decide not to buy, it is customary for the dealer to offer the piece to you at that lowest price again, should you change your mind. However, this is not always the case. If much time has gone by, the dealer may decide that the value of the piece has gone up and refuse to sell it as cheaply as she was formerly willing to do. Sometimes the opposite is true, too; if a dealer holds a piece long enough, she may decide that you are the only one who will buy it at all and may be willing to bargain more favorably. But if you walk away from it the first time, you take your chances. Therefore, always leave the door open to walk back, should you care to.

6. If you decide to buy, the dealer should be willing to give you a sales slip describing the piece in detail, and putting in writing any claims she made for it, such as the *gold content, age, material* it is made of, *size* (in carats) and *identification* of the gem stones, and *appraised value.* On very small or inexpensive pieces you may want these details only for your own information. On expensive pieces, however, such a sales slip should be tucked away with your other valuables. If the piece is stolen, your insurance company may accept it as an appraisal. Or if you ever decide to sell your purchase, the slip will jog your memory. In any case, asking a dealer to put her claims in writing is sobering; what is written down is more likely to be factual than what is casually said. And if it is not factual, and you can prove that, the sales slip should mean that you can get your purchase price back.

By being responsible and businesslike in your behavior, even about such personal pleasures as antique jewelry, you encourage the dealer to be businesslike as well, and ultimately both of you will benefit. However, do be aware that most dealers will not take back anything that is damaged (why should they?) or that you simply have gotten tired of owning—although, the inflation in old jewelry being what it is, some dealers advertise that they will take back anything you buy from them at the price you paid, providing it is in the same condition as when you bought it and they can still resell it at a profit.

At the time of sale, make sure that the dealer wraps your purchase somehow—in tissue paper, a plastic baglet, or a box—so that fragile pieces do not get damaged in your handbag on the way home. Antique jewelry is not only old but often very delicate. If it has survived to get to you, make sure it survives thereafter. I once saw a woman bargain feverishly for a magnificent old cameo, finally come to an agreed price, and then toss her treasure careless-ly into her handbag. The dealer turned white and demanded the piece back; she did not want to sell—at any price—to a barbarian. Some dealers can be barbarians too and not care what happens to a piece when it leaves their hands. But *you do*—so make sure it is wrapped and protected.

7. If you change your mind about a piece you passed up, most dealers will mail it to you very graciously on receipt of a check. Some will cover mailing costs; some will ask you to pay for them. I have found the mails a safe way to receive jewelry, though some dealers warn me that it is best to mail any piece in a large box (which looks more like a tie than a tiepin!) minimally insured. The dealer you do business with will probably have her own method of ensuring delivery.

If you have cause to return a piece, I advise proceeding this way: First, write to (or visit) the dealer and provide a Xerox copy of the original sales slip and evidence as to why you believe the piece is not what it was claimed to be. If the dealer believes you are justified, she may ask you to send the piece back and will refund your money. If the dealer is *not* that reasonable, a second letter with a carbon copy (marked on the original) of the letter sent to the local Antiques Association or Better Business Bureau (or even to the promoter of the antique show at which you bought your piece, or the church or synagogue that ran the show) will usually get fast results. If the dealer still does not respond properly, and you know you are right, you may want to resort to more drastic measures. But I doubt that you would ever have to.

Chapter Two

A Little Bit of History

The historical origins of jewelry lie in *magic, adornment,* and *wealth.* Old books tell us that our ancestors believed in the magical properties of certain gemstones—sapphires stood for honesty and chieftainship, for example, and there are stories of sapphires that turned darker or lost their color if lies were told or if the wearer was in poor health. Amethysts were thought to be a charm against drunkenness, diamonds meant purity, and so on. We retain this "magical" idea about gemstones in our own birthstone legends.

During the Middle Ages, rings that guarded against cramp were popular, motto rings abounded, amulets were worn to guard against everything from witchcraft to sore throats. In those times only royalty or nobility were allowed to wear fine jewelry, and it was not until the rise of the middle class in Europe during the Renaissance that the wearing of fine jewelry spread to more "common" folk. The Romans put golden "fertility" rings on the fingers of their boy babies, and the Victorians put coral or amber beads around their babies' necks; the magic invoked was pretty much the same.

The Victorians were full of "magic," and so their jewelry abounds in symbols, lucky charms, and "talisman" words or ideas. Take the "Regard" ring, a Victorian fancy, for example. The gemstones in the ring spell out the word *Regard:* *R*uby, *E*merald, *G*arnet, *A*methyst, *R*ose Quartz, and *D*iamond, or perhaps the word "Dearest" or a beloved's name. These rings are most usually hoop rings set with different colored stones; only if you know their secret can you read "Regard." But I have seen them with the stones on small gold knots or between pearls. Isn't this like our own contemporary fashion of "Mother" rings (with a stone for each child's birth date) or "Tree of Life" pins—or even our charm bracelets (which the Victorians, too, fancied)?

1. **Hoop ring**

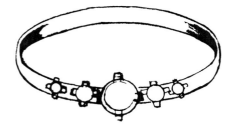

Part of the pleasing quality of Victorian jewelry is this very "magic," this sentiment. Hearts and flowers and lovebirds abound—and ivy ("I cling for life," in *The Language of Flowers,* which every young, romantic, nineteenth-century girl knew), and mizpah (a biblical word: "God watch between me and thee when we are absent one from another"—very popular on turn of the century rings, pins, and lockets). *All* the symbols of binding love (the knot, buckle, bow, rope, and so on) and innocence (angels, babies, pure white coral or ivory or enamel) were popular. Hair jewelry is typically Victorian, worn in the form of rings, pins, earrings, beads, crosses, watch chains, bracelets—an incredible creativity with a very unlikely material!

Snakes were very special to the Victorians, too. Queen Victoria's betrothal ring was a snake with his tail in his mouth—a symbol for eternal life— and the idea was used over and over in Victorian jewelry: coiled snakes on rings and pins; beautiful necklaces of snake chain that circled the neck and clasped in front, tail to head, often with a small heart or heart-shaped locket hanging from the serpent's mouth; and bracelets of a similar design. Though the snake is one of the most universal motifs in jewelry—you will see it in Greek gold, Egyptian adornments, and on the counters of Tiffany's today— these Victorian snakes had a special charm. They were plump, graceful, and often *smiling*—their dolphinlike heads sparkling with diamond or ruby or garnet eyes, their mouths sometimes open to show small sharp teeth.

Most of this charming old jewelry is painstakingly made and carefully finished. A craftsman's wages were low in the nineteenth century, and so hours and hours of work could be lavished on even a modest piece of jet or silver or gutta-percha. Quality workmanship was taken for granted, and jewelry was made to last; people owned less and wore their few good things longer. This high level of workmanship is found only in top-quality jewelry today, if at all. But to the people of earlier times, it was the expected standard. It was only toward the latter part of the nineteenth century, when machine work replaced much of the hand labor, that the quality of workmanship went down. And, even then, there were plenty of jewelry makers—and jewelry wearers—(most notably the devotees of Art Nouveau) who insisted that handcrafting was part of the "magic."

Jewelry as adornment is too familiar an idea to need much explanation. However, it is interesting to explore what specific facts we can learn about the people who came before us, from the ways they used their jewelry to adorn themselves.

Early in the nineteenth century, before Victoria came to the throne of England, the feminine ideal was a slim, romantic, pale sprite. Costume was simple and light; the empire waist, high and girlish, dominated fashion. So much was this light, wraithlike look valued that women drenched their flimsy muslin dresses in water and dried them clinging to the body. (Some women died of pneumonia for their vanity.) The look was "classical"—draped simple fabric, shepherdess curls, girlish simplicity. And the jewelry was equally light and "classical"—cameos; delicately filigreed gold; light, hollow chains; simple, graceful designs.

As the century wore on, and Victoria's influence—solid, stable, down to earth—made itself felt, the ideal of feminine beauty (and thus of costume and jewelry) began to take on a different aspect. Heavier fabrics, more solid and dignified designs, richer and heavier stones and colors dominated. By 1860— the time of the American Civil War—women were covered up in shawls, high collars, long sleeves, and hoopskirts. They wore large pins at the throat, long earrings, heavy bracelets, and substantial, heavily worked gold rings. In 1861, Albert, Victoria's consort, died, and the Queen went into unrelieved mourning. Mourning became a national style, with onyx and jet jewelry widely worn. Meanwhile, women saw themselves as more effective in the world; they espoused social doctrines, they learned new professions, they agitated for more rights. And the aspect of the jewelry changed too; it became assertive and dignified rather than girlish and romantic—massive rather than delicate. The emotional quality, represented by the hearts and bows and flowers, was overt, bold, and unashamed. Then, in the last decade of the century, the mood changed. The dignity turned to "Gibson Girl" delicacy and unreality. Jewelry changed too, to thinness, lightness. Colored stones, enameling, and heavy goldwork all were out of style; diamonds, pearls, and moonstones on the thinnest of bands, the slenderest of chains, were fashionable, and, along with them, the fantastical and flowing "Art Nouveau" designs. Around 1900, jewelry—and women's image of beauty—was at once fragile and sexual, remote and romantic.

The next change in jewelry, and in the idea of beauty, came after the First World War with Art Deco: geometric, bold, sophisticated, mechanistic, architectural, without "romance" or secrets. Jewelry was *flapper;* flappers were flamboyant, streamlined, unsentimental, and so was their adornment. Curves were replaced by straight lines. The delicate white-gold filigree settings for rings and pins of the decade before gave way in the twenties to chunky, angular, straight-line simplicity. For a time the two overlapped, as is always the case in jewelry design. New ideas move slowly. People keep their jewelry for a long time, and really good ideas are repeated over and over. But by the thirties and forties, Art Deco was established. With the Second World War, this look went out and a new fluid, sculptural look dominated. Because it is representative of an earlier time (though hardly "antique" or even very old), Art Deco is collected, too, and collectible.

Jewelry as investment is as old a tradition as jewelry for magic or for adornment. Gold and precious stones have signified wealth in every society; they are mentioned in the Bible, treasured in the pyramids, valued by the Romans, the Scythians, the Greeks. Navaho Indians adorned themselves (and their wives) with silver and turquoise. Indian rajahs put rubies in the foreheads of their idols and the ears and navels of their wives and concubines. Emigrants from Europe to America sewed diamonds in their clothing—even in the babies' diapers—to ensure their start in the new land. And every year, at the big auction houses like Sotheby Parke Bernet and Christie's, jewelry changes hands not only for love of beauty, but for *investment,* in an unstable and unreliable world.

It stands to reason that anything which takes some of its value from being old will only increase in value as it gets older. Antique jewelry, all other things being equal, increases in value as time goes on, and it has proved to be a good investment. But—and this "but" is crucial—it must be the *right* antique jewelry. To be specific: *Only perfect, unmended, mint-condition pieces have, as a general rule, any resale value whatsoever.* Some dealers are fond of explaining away dents, lead solders, and other major flaws in jewelry with this kind of bromide: "If you were as old as this, you wouldn't be perfect either." True—but irrelevant. Though dealers can—and do—sell many pieces that are far from perfect, you—a collector who, if you sell, will probably sell back to a dealer—are fooling yourself if you imagine that a flawed piece will bring you anything like the price you paid for it. IF YOU ARE BUYING FOR INVESTMENT, DO NOT BUY ANYTHING BUT THE BEST Perfect antique jewelry is always eagerly sought after. Broken bits and pieces are always a drug on the market.

Unless you are extremely knowledgeable (and few of us know enough never to be fooled), always buy from a reputable dealer, and get another on-paper opinion or appraisal before making a major purchase for investment. This is not bad advice for any antique jewelry purchase, but for investment buying it is a *must.* Make sure that the dealer you buy from certifies *in writing* everything he or she tells you about the piece, and then put sales slip, appraisal, and a photograph of the piece into your bank vault and leave it there. When the time comes to sell, you will be glad you have this "pedigree."

Do not buy a piece for investment that needs repair, and do not do any repairing, rebuilding, replacing of stones—*anything*—or the piece may lose value. Sometimes a well-meaning jeweler, asked to do a small job on an old piece, will suggest—for safety—the rebuilding of a setting, replacement of old worn pieces, or even (horrors!) putting a new safety catch on an old brooch. This kind of repair, undertaken in good faith, can conservatively *cut the value of the piece in half.* "Perfect" means "in its original condition," not "repaired so as to be perfect." I do not even so much as *size* a ring—though this is a personal feeling and not usually considered important. But some rings cannot be sized without losing enameling, marks, engraving, and definition of the carving, and these should *not* be sized. (If you do size down, ask your jeweler to return the recovered gold to you; it is probably worth more than the cost of the sizing!)

In many cases, in order to make repairs the jeweler must take stones out of their mountings, and in Georgian mountings, for example, or mountings where the stone is surrounded rather than held by prongs, this can only be done in a way that diminishes the value of the piece. Foiled stones cannot be cleaned, except by the most artful specialists in antique repair, without showing the scars of having the stones removed; but only untouched, mint pieces are of top value! Therefore, as much as you possibly can, avoid any repair, replacement, or work of any kind on old pieces if you would *protect* their *investment value*. Above all, never let a jeweler lead-solder a piece of gold jewelry. This immediately puts the piece in another category—a "fixed" piece that has been carelessly, unlovingly handled, and therefore is worth drastically less. (This stricture against touching old pieces applies even to old watches; don't even have them cleaned unless you must. The less they are handled, the better.)

Special care has to be taken of certain materials to keep them in top condition, and therefore at top value. Pearls should be worn periodically and, when the string gets dirty or loose, should be cleaned and restrung. They should not be stored in airtight plastic, or even in the vault for long periods of time without being exposed to air. Perfume, hairspray, cosmetics, and all acids are bad for pearls; when you wear them, remember this. Opals are fragile, and should not be exposed to extreme heat or cold; and if not worn frequently, close to the body, they should be given an overnight bath of glycerine and water, or oiled with a mild oil, from time to time. Ivory, too, is delicate, sensitive to heat and cold and to humidity. No jewelry with stones should be kept in cotton; it should be wrapped in tissue paper, or—and this is by far the best—kept in boxes. (And please, if you are lucky enough to get a piece in its original box, treasure the box as much, almost, as the jewelry, and pass it on in the same way; the value is enhanced.)

Pairs of anything are worth more than twice as much as singles—for example, a pair of bangle bracelets would be worth more (and should not be separated) than two single bracelets of the same quality. The same rule would apply to a parure (set) of jewelry. Collections are, in general, worth more than the sum of the pieces. Signed or dated pieces are, in general, valued more highly than those that are not marked in this way.

A piece signed with Castellani's mark, for example, would be worth many times what a comparable unsigned piece would sell for. Even a lesser-known goldsmith's mark, or anything that is indicative of the history of a piece—a photograph that shows it being worn, a dated note from a former owner, a diary entry describing how it was first given—enhances its value and should be kept as part of the purchase and sold with the piece.

Watches are of small worth if they do not run. Except for really rare and exquisite old pieces, a broken watch is almost valueless, and few watchmakers will agree to put a "dead" antique watch back in working order. Parts are hard or impossible to find, the work is time-consuming and very expensive, and watchmakers are afraid of causing more damage to the old, fragile "patient" and are reluctant to assume responsibility for it. If you have an old watch in good running order, be sure to wind it (but not to overwind it) from time to time to keep it "alive." Remember, too, that many old watches were not antimagnetic, and if they come in contact with a source of magnetic force they will go haywire. This magnetism is a simple matter to fix, but alarming if you don't know what has suddenly caused your old watch to go insane!

In short, if you are buying old jewelry for investment, the very best thing to do is *buy a perfect, unrepaired piece* (preferably a signed and/or marked piece) at a fair price, from a reputable dealer who will back up in writing all claims for it, have a reliable appraiser fortify the dealer's statement, and then put the piece away, or wear it with great care—and maintain it in the same perfect condition in which you bought it. Hold it, wait for the market to rise as it has predictably done for years, and then sell it, preferably retail (not to a dealer) at a healthy profit.

There is one major problem in buying antique jewelry for investment. Nobody has ever loved a stock or bond. But if your jewelry has all the qualities mentioned above, you *will* love it, if you are human. And it is very hard to *sell* a thing you love.

Nevertheless, it does have this potential: unlike a dress or a mink coat or a set of bedroom furniture, antique jewelry is always worth something on resale, and it is comforting to know that your treasure could help one of your children through college, clothe or feed you, or even pay the rent if the need were there.

Chapter Three

What You Can Buy and Where You Can Buy It

If you live in a big city and you love antique jewelry, all the world is spread before you. The yellow pages of your telephone directory will turn up, under the heading "Antiques," shops that specialize in antique jewelry. Usually, the heading "Jewelry" will also furnish you with a few leads. Jewelry stores that sell modern jewelry also sometimes carry "estate" jewelry—that is, the jeweler will buy or take in trade used rings, pins, watches, chains, or what have you. Or perhaps he will buy jewelry from old customers as a service to them, to furnish them with a little ready cash for other things. I have found this last source—the local jeweler who handles estate jewelry—to be a rich source of beautiful old things. Often the jeweler does not really understand or appreciate old jewelry, and therefore, if your eye is sharp, you can locate treasures that to him may seem to be just junk. The occasional jeweler who does love old jewelry will probably be pleased to find an aficionado, and be willing to show you with great pleasure all the antiques he has collected in the past few years.

Shopping the local jewelry stores can make visiting a new town a treat for the antique jewelry hunter, but it is *not* for beginners. Jewelers seem less willing to spend their time talking about old jewelry than antique dealers, who know it serves their own interests to spend their time educating you. If you *do* know your stuff, however, jewelry shops may be richly rewarding. The local jeweler may know whether an old watch can really be repaired and at what specific cost, or whether an old stone is ready to fall out. In other words, he may well know the details about repair and condition that the antique dealer– jeweler may be disinterested in or may "forget" to tell you. This does not in any way contradict what was said before: Do not buy a piece that needs repair, or have a piece repaired, and expect it to retain its full value.

Watch repairmen can be a wonderful source for old watches. Like everybody else, they love the things that—to them—mean quality in their own profession. I have seen fine watches sold for very reasonable sums in watch repair shops. I have also bought interesting old watch fobs and chains from watch repairmen, who had taken them in along with an odd lot of watches and had never had anyone ask for them before. But again, this is rather advanced looking, and you have to know what you are after because these things do not represent a big profit for the watch repairman. He is probably turning them over to you for little more than he paid for them, and therefore is not willing to spend too much time explaining them to you.

Another source of old jewelry (although it becomes less rewarding as it is more thoroughly mined) is the thrift shop, secondhand shop, Junior League shop—the kind of place where a rich lady might send her old jewelry to be pawed over and sold for whatever it's worth. Usually it is worth very little, but now and then you will find something that is worth a lot. I have bought beautiful Victorian combs of jet or amber, or even of silver, from such sources. I have also found wonderful mechanical pencils with patent dates in the 1890s, old mesh bags of brass or silver, and some beautiful old gutta-percha buttons—if gutta-percha can be considered beautiful. These are of course more modest collectibles, but they please me, and I'm sure that if you can pick them up at a reasonable price they will please you, too. Be careful in such places not to buy junk, but to remember the ten questions about quality from chapters four and five. Be as stringent in applying the questions to a piece of modest jewelry as you would be to a piece of Georgian gold. You may choose to buy a piece that does not measure up, anyhow, but remembering the questions will keep you in practice; and if you're giving these modest old collectibles as gifts, you will be able to tell the person who receives them what they are—and what they aren't. One thing to be said for thrift shops and the like: you rarely find a "reproduction" there!

I have friends who frequent garage sales and flea markets in the hope of antique jewelry bargains. The bargains are few, but on a nice day with the sun shining the flea market is a pleasant place to spend an afternoon, and there have been some wonderful finds reported from that source too.

Old jewelry sometimes comes to you through friends, *their* friends, and especially their friends' *mothers* and *grandmothers*. Very often people will own and want to sell old jewelry that for them has little value, but to you may be a treasure. They may be shy about going to dealers because they are overawed or perhaps fear to be misled. They may not know the value of what they have but may be anxious to learn. I always encourage anybody I know who has old jewelry to show it to me. It increases my knowledge, and I can often tell them things they don't know about it. If it's for sale, perhaps I'll want to buy it or perhaps I can steer them to somebody who does.

The primary source for antique jewelry is usually the most obvious—the antique shop. For really fine jewelry, there is no doubt that you will probably see more and do better at a shop that specializes in old jewelry, a shop where the owner knows, loves, respects, and understands what she is selling. This is also the shop in which you will pay market price—hopefully no more, but certainly no less. If you are lucky enough to have a shop like that in your town, get to know the owner and spend as much time with her as you can. A dealer like this is a wellspring of information. It's her business to study old jewelry, know what there is to be known about it, be aware of the reproductions that are in the market, and not to sell you a "repro" for the real thing. And it's the dealer's business to make a friend of you and a future client. The more she educates you, the better customer you'll be, and the quicker you'll be to snap up the really marvelous things she may come upon in her own buying. However, many antique dealers do not see things this way and will not give you the kind of time you would like to look, browse, ask questions, touch, handle, turn over. You will have to evaluate your own subject here and decide whether or not your eager interest will be welcomed. Of course, a small purchase now and then does "sugar" the relationship, although many dealers were most generous with me when I was a young collector, and expected nothing more of me than that I look with the eyes they gave me. Realistically, though, there is no doubt that your welcome in most shops will be warmer if you are a real customer and not just a "looker." I have rarely bought a *bargain* in an antique jewelry store, though I have bought many things that I would have loved at any price. Still, it is only reasonable to understand that somebody who is in the business knows the value of what he or she is selling and will price it accordingly. Wouldn't you?

If a bargain is your objective, you may do better in the general antique shop, where the owner has many kinds of merchandise for sale. In particular, in the shop where jewelry is not a specialty, and the owner may have picked some up in a stray lot, he or she may sell it to you for much less than you'd pay where the dealer is more knowledgeable and more in love with jewelry. Often very respectable rings, bracelets, pins, and chains can be bought from jewelry cases in antique stores, but rarely is the unique piece bought this way. A really fine piece will generally find its way into the hands of a jewelry specialist. Realize also that small shops, flea markets, and thrift shops are *sources* for dealers who get their own stock this way, and if there is something very special it may have been "creamed off" before you ever get there. However, don't be discouraged. If you have the time and the taste for bargains, and some knowledge about what you are buying, you may come up with real wonders.

What kinds of old jewelry are you likely to find? Again, there is a real difference between what you will see in an *antique jewelry store* where the dealer has rifled the world to show you a variety of merchandise, the *general antique shop* where the dealer has somehow "come by" some jewelry, and the *"bargain" spots:* flea markets, garage sales, and so on. In a general antique shop you are likely to find things of a generation ago: Art Deco, filigree white gold rings and pins, Czechoslovakian glass beads, sterling silver pins, inexpensive enameled pins, compacts, small pocketbooks—in short all the minor treasures that your own mother might have kept in her bureau drawer.

I think most people are familiar with what *Art Deco* jewelry looks like. The design of jewelry of the 1920s and 1930s generally has a "geometric" look. Its lines are square rather than rounded. The forms are "architectural": squares, triangles, rectangles—simple, brightly colored, nonobjective or stylized. It does not attempt to reproduce naturalistic forms: flowers, birds, trees, faces. Favorite materials for Art Deco jewelry were platinum, white gold, sterling silver, onyx, diamonds, jade, or glass or plastic in the colors of these stones. There is a blocky, "campy" look to much of the Art Deco jewelry that is easy to identify once you have seen a little bit of it. Art Deco is readily available, and if it suits your taste, the best of it is very much worth buying. Because Art Deco is not very old, it is usually in fairly good condition too, and that's a big plus.

Art Deco "collectibles" are just beginning to be widely reproduced. Do be careful of marcasite, which was very popular with our mothers (1920s–30s) and is handsome and inexpensive, but may not be truly old. I have seen marcasite reproduction rings that look very much like the old ones; after all, the old ones were not made so long ago! Marcasite should *always* be on sterling. Real marcasite is, in fact, a stone, and should be carefully faceted and set, *not pasted;* it should never look cast.

Another category of old jewelry that you can usually find quite readily in antique shops is *turn-of-the-century jewelry,* particularly *gold filled* pieces. Many small antique shops hesitate to show you gold jewelry even if they own any, as they are nervous about the possibility of being robbed. Often if you demonstrate a real interest in old jewelry and then ask if the dealer has anything of finer quality, you will get to see much better pieces that have been tucked away in secret corners in the back or in the safe or cash register. But there are often a few pieces of gold filled jewelry for sale—some old watch chains, or a locket, a watch charm, pins, or even rings. Old gold filled pieces were heavy and durable, not like today's gold plated or gold dipped pieces. "Gold filled," or "rolled gold," meant that sheets of gold were actually wrapped around a core of some other substance (perhaps brass or base metal, sometimes sterling silver). Some of the pieces were hand-chased or hand-engraved—the layer of gold was thick enough to allow this—and they were often guaranteed not to wear through for ten or twenty years, or even for life.

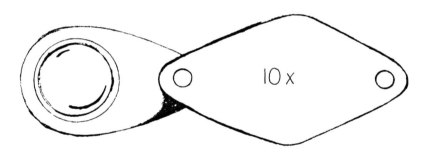

2. Hand-held loupe

You can learn to tell most gold filled jewelry from gold by looking (through the loupe or with a magnifying glass) at the wear spots—links between chains, shanks of rings, and similar areas. If you see any change in color, or places where the gold wore through, you are probably looking at gold filled jewelry. There is an exception, though: sometimes old pieces of gold jewelry were dipped in gold of a higher karat or a different color, and so when the outside layer eventually wore through, the gold beneath would look different. With practice, however, you can tell them apart. Examine all your own pieces carefully with a loupe, and try to recognize the look of gold filled jewelry. Almost always, if a dealer tells you she "doesn't know" if a piece is gold, *it isn't;* it's gold filled (or worse, plain yellow base metal or brass).

A great deal of gold filled jewelry from about 1900 seems to be surfacing in antique shops lately. Only a few years ago, prices on gold filled jewelry were very low; you could pick up a good watch chain with all its charms, bars, and swivels for two or three dollars—perhaps even less. But today, with the high price of gold and silver and the wildly increased interest in old jewelry, the same chain might sell for thirty or forty dollars. So pieces that would have been overlooked a few years ago, or considered not worth cleaning up to sell, are now sought after. A great deal of gold filled jewelry was made around 1900, and often it was styled to look exactly like the more expensive gold

3. **Eye loupe**

jewelry of the day. So you will find it in abundance in antique shops, and—if you like it and it passes the tests in chapters four and five—it is well worth buying and will probably give you long and faithful wear. (If the gold does wear through, the piece can be replated; but modern replating simply deposits a thin film of gold over the surface below, and will never look or wear the way the layer of gold originally pressed onto gold filled jewelry did.)

Another turn-of-the-century fancy that often surfaces in antique stores is the *lavaliere.* This is a delicate pendant often of gold, often with gemstones or pearls, that our mothers and grandmothers wore around the neck. Lavalieres are light and delicate, and have an Art Nouveau quality. They were worn around 1900 and are often very beautiful, but they do not look good with today's dresses and so are often passed over; therefore they are available in abundance and priced well. If you like them, they can be a "best buy."

Ivory beads; glass beads; jet pins, beads, earrings, and lockets; tortoise and gutta-percha lockets, chains, and crosses—all of the more modest jewelry materials (what was, in fact, considered "costume" jewelry when it was bought and worn) often show up in antique shops.

Another old favorite item is the small portrait pin. These were popular for a number of years, from the turn of the century onward. They were rarely framed in gold; almost always they were gold filled or base metal. When they are in nice condition, with the frame unbroken and the photograph clear, they are really pleasing, modest old treasures. Some of the pictures are quite wonderful. I have babies, fat old ladies, mustachioed men—and I like them all. The price should be low: I bought mine from $2.00 to $12, never more. The frames are often ingenious and different, and if you like people, portrait pins can make a wonderful collection.

Although everything old seems to be "collectible," I would not recommend buying yellow metal or white metal Art Deco jewelry, which was five-and-ten jewelry in its time. It will not stand up well, usually was not very well designed, was not intended to be worn a long time, was mass-produced, and does not—for me, at least—have any of the charm I find in older jewelry or better jewelry. What is collectible now is Art Deco *plastic* jewelry, and it probably will become more so. Plastic bracelets, buttons, pins, and belt buckles with Art Deco motifs seem to have more integrity in the design and material than base metal pieces of the same style, and if they appeal to you, by all means hunt them down now—before they become scarce and expensive.

In the 1920s (the flapper era) long beads and pendants, tassle necklaces, and oriental novelties were fashionable, and often you can find these in antique shops. I have some beautiful Peking glass beads that are held together with hand-crocheted motifs of silk. They were surely made in China and look smashing with today's fashions. Amber beads were popular in the 1920s too. Indeed, they have been popular for a long time in almost every culture. The 1920s amber beads are readily available, although the prices on them have

skyrocketed in recent years. Faceted ambers, cherry ambers that look like red
marbles, strands of golden ambers, perhaps interspersed with other beads—all
these may be found hanging on antique shop racks. Another old favorite that
has become very popular is what my mother called "crystals." My mother's
"crystals" were made of glass. They were faceted, beautiful, clear, and brilliant—but they were glass. Some crystals, however, are really made of *crystal*—
that is, clear quartz *stone*—and these "real crystals" are worth at least four
times as much as the glass "crystals." You can easily distinguish one from the
other. The glass "crystals" are warmer to the touch; clear rock crystal is cold,
like all stones. Touch your tongue to the crystals before they have warmed up
from your hands, and you will easily note the difference in temperature. Stone
is harder than glass, too. If you click glass "crystals" against your teeth, there
is a different feel from clicking rock crystal against your teeth. Try this if you
have both available to you—you will readily know which is which. The most
conclusive test is to look at the place in the bead where the string shows
through. Rock crystal is doubly refractive—that is, the line of the string will
appear to be doubled when you look at it through the bead. Glass is *not* doubly
refractive, and so you will always see only a single line of string. If a dealer
tries to sell you "real crystals" and they turn out to be glass, it is probably not
worth your time to explain why they are not real crystal. Buy them if you like
them and the price is right. If you come across a string of real rock crystals,
you are in luck. Beads of rose quartz (which is pinky cloudy quartz) were also
loved in this period and are also available today. (Most dealers *do* seem to
know the difference between rose quartz and pink glass.)

A word of caution about *glass beads:* many new glass beads are being sold
in antique shops because they "look old." It takes a little expertise to know
which is which. The old ones often have brass connectors. Many Czechoslovakian beads were made this way, and these brass-and-glass treasures are often
beautiful to wear and fun to own. Many old glass beads imitated more expensive natural materials—jade, rock crystals, ambers, amethysts, garnets, opals.
The new beads may be so shameless as to be *plastic,* in which case I would not
give them houseroom.

Another word of caution: Many plastic beads are being sold as *amber.*
Real amber has a very distinctive look and feel when you know it, but until
you are sure, there are a few simple tests that you can perform. Like a paternity test, they will give you only negative evidence; they will not tell you definitely that a piece *is* amber, but will certainly tell you if it is *not.* Amber is
electric. If you rub amber on a woolen skirt or on your hair, and then put it
close to a tiny piece of tissue—a really tiny piece—the tissue will jump up onto

the amber and be magnetized. If a necklace is offered to you as amber and it does not have this electricity, pass it by; it is not amber. However, plastics have been made that can be electrically charged this way, and so the fact that a necklace does pick up tiny pieces of tissue does not *guarantee* that it is amber. Some jet has this property too, although not as strikingly as amber, but jet beads will sometimes do the same trick. Glass beads never will.

Amber also has a distinctive feel—a kind of fatty, soft, greasy feel, and it is very light: it will float on salt water (though few dealers I know will fill up a basin for you to try it). It is warm to the touch, much warmer than glass, and is uneven in color. It is a natural material, after all, the exudate of trees, and often has bits of organic material (even bugs) in its interior. Hold your "amber beads" up to the light. If they are extremely even in color, be a bit suspicious. The nicest kind of amber beads to buy are those that still have their original clasp, which almost always was an amber clasp that screws together. Check strands of amber beads carefully to see if any beads are missing; make sure that, if they are graduated, the beads match; if there are inclusions of other beads, be sure that everything that *should* be there *is* there.

If the beads you like are glass and brass, check them to make sure that none of the elements is missing, that everything matches, that the brasses are not broken or twisted or bent, that all the parts are original, and that the clasp matches the brass between the beads in color and style. Old beads of all kinds are readily available in most antique shops. The prices are usually modest, and many of the materials are fascinating and unique. If you like them, they are a good buy, and most of them will become more collectible—and expensive—as time goes on and they become more rare.

Jet beads are a good example of this. Jet has been known since early times and has been found in Bronze Age burial sites in Britain, but it is especially associated with nineteenth-century mourning jewelry. After Prince Albert died and Queen Victoria went into mourning, only mourning jewelry was worn at the English court for some thirty years. That meant that black materials—jet, onyx, bog oak, black enamel on gold—were extremely popular. After the Queen began to wear silver jewelry at court (in the 1880s) the jet craze began to fade, and by the 1930s the Whitby jet mines, where the finest jet was dug out of the ground like coal, had closed down. There is still a great deal of jet jewelry to be had—beads, pins, pendants, lockets, bracelets, earrings—and all of it old and authentic if it really is jet. Sometimes black glass was used for the same kind of jewelry and called "French jet." But glass is colder to the touch than jet, is heavier, and it has a different look: jet is coal-like in appearance, almost "greasy" in feel (rather like amber), and is

softer but less easily fractured than its glass counterpart. It is never translucent, and some jet has a slight electricity, similar to amber.

Jet—like amber—is an *organic* material. It is the result of great pressure
and heat in the earth's crust acting on buried vegetative matter and wood. Jet
is, in fact, a first cousin of coal. It is not hard to tell jet and glass apart once
you have seen a few examples of each, but be wary if you have not. All that's
black and glitters is not Victorian jet.

Ivory has a soft flat finish (it looks as though it were waxed) and, when it
is old, it ages to a soft beige color that many people prize. But most important,
ivory has graining. True elephant ivory has crosshatched graining—very light
little intersecting brownish lines that enhance its beauty. If the beads or carvings that are shown to you do not have this graining, don't accept them as
elephant ivory. Vegetable ivory, which comes from certain tropical nuts, also
sometimes has graining, but it is quite different—straight lines or perhaps
rows of dots. The appearance of this vegetable ivory is different from the
appearance of elephant ivory, too. It is drier looking, without ivory's distinctive waxy gloss. It is usually white, though some unscrupulous people dip
pieces in tea to make them look "aged."

Bone, which is often beautifully carved, also looks different from elephant
ivory. It has a white, very dry look and lacks the waxy, buttery gloss and
characteristic graining of ivory. Many beautiful beads and carvings have been
done in bone, and there is nothing wrong with it. Ivory, however, is generally
considered more beautiful and desirable, and is therefore more expensive.
Make sure that if you are being offered "ivory" it *is* ivory.

Ivory is a laminated material, and if it is soaked in water it tends to crack
and break. So if you buy ivory beads that are dirty, *never* soak them in soapy
water to get them clean. They can be washed very carefully with a Q-tip and
soapy water or a damp rag, but be sure to dry them immediately, and *don't get
the string wet.* A wet string in contact with ivory beads for the hour it takes the
string to dry can split them in half. If ivory is left out in the sun, it will bleach,
and many people who dislike the beige color of old ivory will whiten it by this
means. Peroxide will whiten it a bit, too, but again—never, never, soak it. If
ivory cracks or warps or loses its glossiness through age or misuse, very little
can be done to restore it, so it is important to buy ivory in good condition and
to keep it that way. Ivory is also extremely sensitive to heat and humidity. If
you have fine ivory pieces, store them in a cool dry room, out of direct sunlight.

You may at some time find a piece marked "French Ivory." French ivory
is plastic, not ivory at all. It is generally easy to tell the difference between

ivory and plastic simply by looking and touching. If you own a piece that you are not sure of, this test will help you determine whether it is ivory or plastic: First, choose a tiny area on the piece that will not be spoiled by a small amount of abrasion. Next, using a nailfile and holding the piece up very close to your nostrils, rub the tiny area with the nailfile—and sniff. If the piece is ivory (or bone), it will smell like burning hair. If the piece is plastic, it has an acrid sharp smell, a bit like sour milk. Be very cautious when you make this test. It is never worth spoiling a beautiful piece, no matter what it's made of, to authenticate the material.

Tortoise is another jewelry material that you may well find in antique shops. Tortoise combs, pins, pendants, chains, earrings, and even rings were plentiful in the nineteenth century. Victorians were very fond of it, and even used it for boxes, toilet sets, and what have you. In the early nineteenth century, beautiful *piqué work* was made from tortoise inlaid with gold and silver. The metal was actually melted into the tortoise with heat and pressure, and patterned into flowers and leaves and—later—little gold stars, balls, or crisscrosses of metal. Fine tortoise jewelry is becoming harder to find, and prices have jumped accordingly. Beautiful long tortoise earrings that date back to the 1850s could be bought only a few years ago for $10 or $15. They are now selling for $75, if you can find them. Tortoise bracelets, usually wide cuffs, are still inexpensive when you find them. But be careful: they are brittle and likely to break easily. Tortoise becomes dull with age and wear. Like other organic materials, it is sensitive to heat and humidity, and if it has been kept in a hot or dry place (like an attic), it dries out and becomes very fragile. The dryness and dullness sometimes can be helped by a good bath in mineral oil. Actually lay the piece in the oil for a day or two, to help restore its suppleness and luster. Robert Arnold, Senior Conservator at the Metropolitan Museum of Art, suggests polishing tortoise back to its original luster, but this should be done only by an expert who knows how to handle the material. As an amateur, you can try the oil bath followed by a light waxing.

Often the backs of tortoise pins are loose, since the metal was put directly into the tortoise shell itself. This can be helped with a little glue, although, as with everything else, a perfect piece that does not require gluing is preferable to one that needs first aid. Look carefully at piqué pieces and make sure that every bit of the metal that was originally set into the tortoise is still there. If you are buying piqué earrings, check to see if the original wires are still on them, and make sure that the two earrings match. Sometimes earrings that came in sections have been broken and somebody has "creatively" added or taken away some parts.

Plastic "tortoise" is fairly common, and so it is a good idea to know how to tell the difference. The same test described for ivory can be used for tortoise. Pick a spot that will not mar the appearance of the piece, carefully file the tortoise close to your nostrils, and then sniff. Tortoise, an organic material too, smells like burning hair. Plastic smells like plastic. You can also often tell tortoise from plastic simply by holding it up to the light. Plastic is generally fairly even in color and pattern; tortoise never is. Think of the difference between formica and wood. That is often the difference between the look of plastic and tortoise. *All* old tortoise will probably show some wear. Plastic rarely does. Plastic was molded and may show mold lines. Tortoise was steamed and bent, very much as bentwood chairs are made today, and so it has a different look. If you buy a tortoise locket, make sure (as with all lockets) that the hinge is tight, the closure is secure, and the original frames are in. The findings in tortoise were placed into the tortoise itself, and therefore are not always secure. Many heavy old jet lockets look something like tortoise— but not if you hold them up to the light. Tortoise is translucent, and you will always see some light through it.

Another material you may find in antique shops is *gutta-percha.* Some antique dealers don't know what it is and will give you fanciful explanations about it; but you should learn to know gutta-percha and, if you can, to love it. It is a material not much in demand now, but it is authentic to the period, is not being reproduced, is very cheap to buy, and will probably skyrocket in value within the next ten years, just as tortoise did.

What does gutta-percha look like? It's a dark brown or brownish-black material rather light in weight, soft in its luster, molded rather than carved— a rubberlike material with a klunky kind of charm all its own. I own a gutta-percha watch chain with small circles of gold around every link. I have gutta-percha and leather clasps that may have come off a Civil War cape, gutta-percha pins, bracelets, and even gutta-percha earrings. Gutta-percha is not everybody's cup of tea, but if it is yours, and you collect it, you will not be sorry.

Another material similar to gutta-percha and often mistaken for it is *bog oak.* Bog oak is actually a kind of peat. It looks a lot like wood, dark brown and with a slight grain usually showing on the back surface. Bog oak was native to Ireland, and was carved, not molded. The Irish were very proud of their bog oak jewelry, and nearly always carved a harp, a castle, or a shamrock on it. So if you have a strange-looking woody piece with one of those symbols as part of the motif, you may indeed have bog oak. I have seen it in bracelets, buttons, pins, and even in magnificent pin-and-earring sets embellished with gold. It is

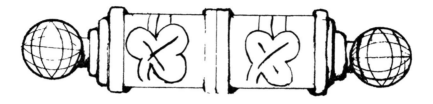

4. Bog oak

absolutely and without question Victorian. Nobody would bother to reproduce it today. Dealers often don't know what it is when they get it, and will sell it for fifty cents or a dollar. Buy it if you like it: it will someday be worth much more!

Perhaps you have seen a bluish-black metal made up into chains, or watches, or watch pins, or small mesh bags. This is *gunmetal*. Some of the little bags may even be stamped "Gunmetal" or "French Gunmetal." These were popular around the turn of the century. They are inexpensive to buy and sometimes very pretty. Gunmetal, too, is not being reproduced as of this writing, and so when you buy it you are buying something that is truly old and fun to wear. Gunmetal has few problems except rust. If a piece is badly neglected it will turn rusty, and there is very little you can do to get it back to the original finish. You can try rubbing it with a little fine steel wool and then waxing it or oiling it, or polish it with a good chrome polish. But if the bluish color has gone, it will not come back. Try to buy gunmetal that is in good condition. The mesh bags are often ripped or broken in the corners. It is possible to "knit" mesh together if you are very handy, but I have never been able to do it successfully, and so I will not buy a mesh bag unless it is perfect.

Coral was another favorite of the Victorians, and many kinds of jewelry are to be found made of orange-red or light pink (angel skin) coral. Mothers sometimes put strings of coral beads around their babies' necks to protect against sore throats. Whether or not they were effective, these small coral necklaces are very attractive, and treasures if you can find them. They are generally made of small round beads (not graduated) with push clasps, and will fit you as a choker if your neck is small. Larger coral bead necklaces are available too, but they may range high in price, as they are most desirable. The larger and more beautifully colored the coral, the more expensive it is. Branch coral necklaces were also popular and are still easy to find, though they may be broken; they do not weather time as well as the round and oval beads. Coral is still being imported from Italy, but the new coral is shiny and has a different look from old coral, which always shows wear. Often new red coral is dyed, and the color is brighter and deeper.

The Victorians also liked flat coral beads assembled into round or half-moon pins or used as earrings. These beads were button shaped and were attached to the pin by small spikes. The beads often came off the spikes, and you may find pieces with buttons off. If you have the buttons, though, they are easily glued back. The pieces should have a soft glow, not a bright shine.

Coral was beautifully carved in the nineteenth century into fruits, flowers, vegetables, cherubs, hands, and the faces of beautiful women. It was used in rings, long earrings, pins, and pendants. The Victorian ladies brought coral home when they went sight-seeing to Italy, or it was imported from Italian carvers.

You are unlikely to mistake coral for any other material, but if you are in doubt, there is an easy test to make sure you own coral and not plastic. Have a magnifying glass ready; with a toothpick, drop a tiny drop of lemon juice on an inconspicuous spot on the coral. Look through the magnifying glass, and you will see little bubbles like champagne bubbles in the lemon juice. Any acid will give you this result with coral, but a strong acid will dissolve the coral—so be careful. (This test will also work with bone and ivory, but you are not likely to mistake them for coral.)

Never drop corals in a jewelry cleaner or subject it to any acid. (That advice also holds good for all natural materials: tortoise, ivory, amber, bone, pearls, and the like.) Acids will injure them, perhaps even destroy them. With amber and pearls, the perfume that you use may spoil them, so never spray on perfume or hair spray after you have donned your amber beads or your pearls.

Use the same care in buying coral beads as you would with any other beads: check to see that no beads are missing and that no foreign beads have been added. Try to find coral beads that are on their original chain or string, with the original clasp if possible. When pins and earrings are made with any wired leaves or fruits, check to see that all the pieces are there, and unbroken. Coral survives extremely well, but many times fragile pieces get lost or broken, and (as with everything else) perfect is best.

How about *hair jewelry*? Well, either it's your thing or it isn't. I like it and have bought a great deal of it because it is very special, it meant a lot to the people who originally wore it, and because it is distinctively Victorian. Hair jewelry can come in a variety of forms—earrings, necklaces, watch chains, beads, pins with hair, rings with hair, pictures made of hair, bracelets made of hair (sometimes with gold clasps). It was a popular art, and the ingenuity of the people who made it was almost unbounded. Watch chains made of hair are quite handsome; they make nice necklaces if you don't mind the scratchiness. Hair rings are often touching memorials of a loved one, and not necessarily a dead loved one, either. Some hair jewelry was made by women at home in an elaborate process that included stripping the hair, forming it into shapes, and restiffening it. Other times, women would simply take a hair sample from a loved one and send it to a jeweler who offered a catalog showing the ways in which it could be mounted.

A hair watch chain or hair beads can be washed in soap and water if you are careful and dry them well. Hair that is enclosed under crystal has to be more carefully treated because if moisture gets underneath the crystal, the hair may mold. Hair rings may not be harmed by water, but they do not dry readily, and long-term dampness is bad for them.

If you buy hair jewelry, make sure that it is perfect, since there is little value or beauty to broken or frayed hair pieces. A little frizzing may be repaired by spraying hairspray directly on the raggedy part and "gluing" it together. But this is only for very minor repairs. In general, if hair jewelry is not in very good condition, pass it by. Some dealers will take the hair out of lockets and pins; I find this as senseless as any other kind of "renovation" of old jewelry. The hair gives the piece character, and is a warm reminder of the strength and uniqueness of human love.

Some beautiful old lockets or pins actually had hair "paintings"—pictures of plumes, feathers, flowers, or memorial urns made with hair. These are often quite beautiful, and I like to leave them as they are, although some people take the hair out and use the lockets for pictures of people they themselves love.

Hair jewelry has gone up greatly in price in recent years, and I'm sure will continue to rise, since it is another of those unique Victorian materials that is not being reproduced.

If you are lucky enough to have a really first-rate antique jewelry store in your town, or in the town you visit, you probably will find a lot of pieces made of the more modest materials that have been described here, plus a wealth of other more costly and sophisticated pieces. More important, you should also find a dealer who knows something about antique jewelry and can teach *you* something!

The First Five Questions to Ask

It has been said—and it's true—that antique jewelry experts may know a lot, but they never stop learning. And even the wisest of them are sometimes fooled by pieces that are not what they seem—or are claimed—to be. Nevertheless, there are a few simple questions that even a novice can use to determine whether a piece is a dud or a possible treasure. No one who loves or buys old jewelry should approach it without knowing what these questions are. So here are the first five:

1. Is it what it's claimed to be?
When something catches your eye and you ask the dealer to show it to you, always ask as well (and *before* you look at the price tag!) what it is: what it's made of; how old it is; what it was used for, if that's not immediately clear; whether all the parts are original; whether the stones are genuine—anything that seems reasonable in determining what the value of the piece might be. When your questions have been answered—then and only then—*look at the price tag.*

Often dealers will not know all the answers, and I am always more impressed if they say, "I don't know" than if they fabricate to please me. If you ask, "Is this gold?" and the dealer answers, "It may be," figure that it isn't. If there were a chance that it might be, it would have been tested; gold is better than dross! But many materials are harder to know. Synthetic stones are often impossible to tell from the real ones without using sophisticated instruments. Many dealers are not able to tell ivory from bone (though when you finish reading this book, *you* will be), tortoise from plastic, coral from glass, and so on.

In any case, listen to the facts about the piece. (Don't bother to ask: "Where did you get it?" That is usually a waste of time and leads to a lot of fiction. Treasure, however, the dealer who tells you the truth on this one!) Then, *silently,* using all your knowledge, try to determine if the piece is as claimed. If it's gold, is it marked? This is not a foolproof test; much gold is unmarked, and recently the market has been flooded with imports marked *18K* that are not even gold. But it is a clue. Does the piece show signs of wear? Gold *never* wears off, but sometimes the Victorians dipped gold jewelry in a higher karat gold or gold of another color, and this overlay might wear off and show the color beneath.

It stands to reason that you will not be able to examine a piece in such detail with your naked eye. Never be abashed to bring a loupe (or magnifying glass) or to ask for the dealer's loupe to help you study a piece carefully. I carry two good loupes—one 4x magnification, the other 10x. They have saved me from missing important flaws in jewelry: prongs missing, enamel chipped, mosaic pieces missing, stones cracked or chipped or replaced—and they have turned up unexpected bonuses as well: marks of origin, dates, inscriptions, hidden catches, and even—in one case—the tiny hairline opening hinting that a simple gold wedding band I held in my hand was a *gemel* (twin ring, one opening up into two). No dealer should object to your studying a piece under a loupe; in fact, many dealers insist that you do, so that you know exactly what you are buying. A few naïve dealers, when they see you handling the jewelry so "expertly," will ask: "Are you a dealer?" Good! They will be much more careful of what they say about the jewelry and more likely to stick to facts if they feel that you "know your stuff."

If a piece is marked something like 1/20 10K, or GF, it is *gold filled*—a layer of gold filled with another metal, probably brass. Gold filled jewelry is often beautiful and wears well, but it is not *solid gold.* "Rolled gold" also is not as good as gold. And "gold plated" or "gold washed" is just base metal with the thinnest film of gold over it. So make sure you are clear about what the dealer means by "gold."

Gold is an "inert" metal; that is, it does not combine chemically with anything. So *high karat* gold does *not tarnish*. (It does wear and dent readily, because it's soft.) If you see much tarnish on "gold" pieces, suspect that they may be very low karat (9 karat, or even lower) or gold filled (brass tarnishes like mad). They may also be dirty; many dealers do not clean their jewelry because they feel dirt adds to the "authenticity"; it *doesn't*. Don't be afraid to ask the dealer about the karat of gold, and to check the piece yourself for marks and for signs of tarnish or wear. Assume that the dealer, like you, wants the piece in question to be "as claimed."

All old gold (unless it is in absolutely mint condition—and this is rare), will show signs of wear. With your loupe, study chains where the links rub against each other, or where the spring ring attaches. Look at the hinges of pins, the shanks and edges of rings. If you see *something else* coming through the gold, the piece is probably gold filled.

Silver is generally easier to identify, as it is more likely to be marked. "Silver" means "sterling silver," as does ".925." But be careful of pieces marked "German silver" or "nickel silver." They may be beautiful, and you may decide to buy them, but they contain *no* silver at all; they are a mixture of nickel and zinc. In all my looking I have never seen a piece of old *silver-plated* jewelry.

There is a great deal of Victorian silver jewelry available, almost all from the latter half of the nineteenth century. Silver was extremely popular in England around 1870; by 1880 the craze had worn off. But in that decade, silver chains; massive lockets; sentimental pins (sometimes with gold inlays) showing hearts, ivy leaves, arrows, forget-me-nots, or lovebirds; heavy silver bangle bracelets; and silver-mounted Scotch agate pins, earrings, jointed bracelets with lock-and-key closing, or lockets were all the fashion. Later in the century, around 1900, silver made a comeback, with smaller "sentimental" pins—sometimes bearing the biblical word *mizpah* (a fad around 1890); cross-heart-and-anchor charms ("faith, hope and charity"); name pins; bar pins with the familiar ivy, arrows, hearts, and flowers; and Victoria "silver anniversary" mementos (1887 was the fiftieth year of her reign) were popular. Besides these more traditional pieces, the Art Nouveau movement, which started in the late nineteenth century and influenced jewelry for nearly four decades, adored silver, and many lovely pieces characteristic of Art Nouveau design are available. However, a caution: many more *reproductions* are available—many of them castings from original old pieces. Beware of these; there is nothing wrong with them if you know they *are* reproductions, but you should not buy them believing that they are old. Some are hard for a beginner to tell from the originals. When in doubt about Art Nouveau (as with anything else), ask the dealer straight out—"Is it old? Is it a repro?" And if the dealer's answer still leaves you in doubt, my advice is that, unless you love it no matter what its pedigree, don't buy it.

Old Russian silver jewelry shows up now and then. The Russians were masters at niello work—silver with blue-black inlay—marked ".625." Buckles, lockets, chains, or watch fobs of niello are particularly nice, and belts and buckles of niello can be magnificent. Don't confuse Russian niello with a similar process from Siam. The Siamese pieces have oriental figures incised in blue-black silver; they are contemporary, common, and not collected as "old" jewelry.

As for stones: *gemstones* are cold to the touch (if you put them to the tip of your tongue, you will feel the difference), as already explained; glass is warmer. Ambers can be clear or cloudy, yellow, orange, red, brown, or even (rarely) green, and will pick up little bits of tissue after you rub them on your hair or a woolen garment. Most gemstones are hard and will not scratch easily, so beware of an "emerald" or "sapphire" that is very worn; it's probably glass. Old corals have a soft, dull finish and soft color; they are not bright and glassy like many of the new dyed ones. Jets look like coal, are often rather coarsely faceted, and are lighter and warmer to the touch than their glass counterparts. (Some dealers tend to call anything that is black "jet," as they call anything that looks-like-but-isn't-gold "pinchbeck." Don't be fooled! Check "pinchbeck" in chapter six and in the glossary.

In short, use every bit of expertise you have to evaluate what you have been told, and if a piece fails your tests and is *not* as claimed, remember that fact when and if price comes up for discussion. Read and reread this book, plus anything else you can get your hands on that will teach you to identify and develop a "feel" for materials and period.

If a piece *is* as claimed—or if it isn't, but you like it anyway—go on to Question 2:

2. Is it in good condition, preferably perfect?
Again, look the piece over carefully. If it's a brooch, I always turn it backside up and check to see if the hinge or catch has been repaired. Look for solder marks, differences in color, a "new"-style hinge (see Illustration 5) on an "old" piece.

Check finger rings to make sure that they have not been improperly sized (with soft solder, which leaves a darker, grayish mark) or are not so worn that they are doomed to crack. Try to move each stone with your fingernail; make

sure that it is tight in its settings—held by the metal and not just glued in—
and that it is reasonably free from chips, scratches, or cracks. My advice is:
don't buy rings that show glue around the settings. Probably the gold was so
worn that the stones could not be held in and so they *had* to be glued. No
matter what you may be told, these stones will eventually fall out and have to
be replaced with more glued-in stones. Pass such rings by. Also check that the
metal in the setting still comes up *over* the stone, or you may buy a perfectly
beautiful old ring, wear it once, and have a blank setting staring up at you.
Look at the stones and settings and try to judge whether they have been
tampered with. Do the stones match well in color and cut? Always check them
in profile. If you see a few high ones and a few low ones, some have been
replaced. Check the prongs. Are any broken off? Do the settings look as
though they have been opened, or were made for stones of another size or
shape? Years ago, when old rings were worth less, stones were often pried out
of them and the settings sold "as is" for old gold. Now, when they are all the
rage, the old rings are sometimes set with new stones and sold as genuine "old"
articles. So study them carefully.

Check old chains to make sure that the links are all original and have not
been repaired, and that they have their original old clasps and swivels ((see
Illustration 25). This is sometimes hard to know, but look, and ask if you
aren't certain. Any old chain, of any material, should show some wear between the links; look for this. Snake chains were sometimes poorly repaired
and have "stiff" places; run a snake chain through your fingers and make sure
that every bit of it is flexible. Check that chains have their original clasps;
sometimes a marked gold spring ring is attached to a chain that is not gold.
Never accept a mark on a clasp as proof of the chain unless you are sure that
both match.

If you are looking at beads, make sure they are all there, with their
original clasps. Ambers, for instance, nearly always came with amber screw
clasps, and ivories with ivory. If there is a pattern of drops or dangles, none of
the pieces should be missing. Beads on their original strings or chains are best.

Be especially cautious when you look at old earrings. Earrings are so
delicate that few perfect ones survive, but many "creative" dealers take pieces
from broken necklaces or what have you and put them on new ear wires. (By
the way, nearly all Victorians had pierced ears.) If you suspect this, ask forth-
rightly about it; usually you will get a true answer to any question you are
knowledgeable enough or brave enough to ask, but many dealers will not tell
you bad news unless they have to. If you are really a "detective," get hold of
a modern catalog of jewelry findings and learn the few basic modern styles of

earring backs. Never buy "old" earrings that sport these new backs!

Any gold piece that has been repaired with lead or "soft" solder (black or silver colored) has been dealt a mortal blow. In time the lead will "eat" through the gold, and the piece will break and probably be irreparable. Soldering with gold solder is the proper way to mend a gold piece, but the gold ("hard") solder melts at a much higher temperature than "soft" solder, and thus must be handled more carefully. Also, if the piece has stones that would crack at high temperatures, a careless jeweler will often use soft solder rather than take the piece apart and do the job right. Beware of lead solder and do not buy a gold piece with a lead repair unless you are really mad for it. The price should reflect that the piece has been shoddily treated and should be *low*.

In general, a piece that has a major flaw or a major repair is worth much less, perhaps half the price of the same piece in mint condition. Be prepared to pay top price for the finest—but be prepared, also, to be firm and know your rights if you are offered a piece that is flawed.

Look to see that the piece is not so worn that it is going to break. Take time to wiggle the pin on brooches and make sure that the hinge will hold and that it closes safely. Beware of anything that needs fixing. Most jewelry repairmen do not know much about old jewelry and dislike working on it. They would rather rebuild it than repair it—and that immediately decreases its value. If the pin is very loose, if the piece has been lead-soldered, if it is broken, cracked, or very worn, my advice is to pass it by.

Be especially wary of the dealer who tries to put you off with something like the old chestnut mentioned earlier—"If you were as old as this piece, you'd be dented too." It's true—but so what? The piece you want is the one that has braved the years undented, the premium piece that's worth owning and treasuring. Sometimes you'll see a piece that really has the blues—but that you love and want anyway. My advice is to put it aside sternly and hope you'll see another one someday that is in good shape and worth buying. Remember: Only a *perfect* (or very close to it) piece has any *sure* (resale) *value*!

If the piece you fancy is in good condition, not dented or out of shape, no parts broken or glued on, no really ugly repairs visible, nothing missing and not put together haphazardly, not scratched or heavily worn, then consider Question 3:

3. Is it genuine?
This is probably the question that is hardest to answer (and the one that scares you most). And yet you really can answer it more often than not if you keep your wits about you. The first step is: *ask the dealer.* Very few dealers can resist

this question asked straight out, eye to eye; most will readily confess, "It's a repro [reproduction]" if it is, or reply "I don't know" if they don't.

If the dealer tells you that the piece is old, or seems unsure, examine it carefully again. Don't be shy; pull out your loupe and study your find shamelessly, for as long as you need to.

Does the piece show wear? Wear is not an absolute proof of age—some Victorians bought jewelry and put it in a drawer, just as we do—but it is very unusual for a truly old piece to show no wear at all.

New pieces of "old" jewelry generally have been *cast,* and often none too carefully, so if your find shows mold marks (fine lines where the edges of the mold met), be wary. In general, distrust anything that is "antiqued." Truly old pieces do not need to be chemically treated to make them look dark in the cracks; they often are dirty or tarnished enough to qualify. Even if they have been polished and shined, be careful of anything that has been purposely darkened to look "antique."

Be respectful of handwork, and look for it—hand carving or engraving, slight irregularities in patterns, pieces where settings were fitted to stones. Our grandfathers had much more time than we do, and hand labor was much cheaper; few reproductions (unless they were carefully crafted to sell at a high price) would be handmade today.

Turn all brooches over and check hinges and catches. (See Illustration 5.) Old ones have long-bar hinges, curved "C" catches, and pins that extend *outside* the edge of the piece. On Art Nouveau made around the turn of the century, you begin to see the "new style" round hinge and safety catch. Victorian pins, however, and of course earlier ones, should all have the old-style hinge and catch illustrated here. (Very old brooches, eighteenth century and older, were sewn to dresses, and they have loops or bars instead of pins; but these are extremely hard to come by.)

Of course gold and silver marks can date a piece, as can the karat of gold and the way it is indicated. (See chapter six, for a complete rundown on marks.) Many old and genuine pieces have no marks at all, though—so marks are a *clue,* but not con*clu*sive.

A good rule of thumb is that inexpensive old jewelry is rarely reproduced because there just is not enough profit in it. The highest-priced pieces offer the incentive, all right, but when *they* change hands, they are often authenticated by experts before the sale is completed; hence, faking them is dangerous. The most fertile field for hanky-panky, then, is in the middle range ($35–$350), and that's where you should be most careful.

The real test of "Is it genuine" lies in your own perception, knowledge,

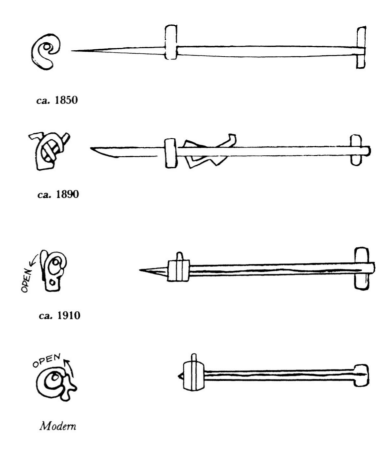

5. The evolution of the brooch pin

and developing taste. The more you see and touch, the more questions you ask, the more you read and study, the better judge you'll be. Victorians had a style all their own; they loved hearts, flowers, arrows, hands, birds, mottoes, hair jewelry, bugs, flies, leaves, fruits. *Everything* had a meaning to them, and they loved sentiments and symbols. They rarely used a straight line if they could manage a curve, or a plain one if they could include a curlicue. They loved *pietra dura* (colored stone) mosaics; "Etruscan" gold pieces that mimicked the style of old Greek treasures; coral (soft orange-red and pale pink angel skin); agates set in gold (rare) or silver; jet, amber, gutta-percha, and tortoise. They were especially fond of snakes and used them in everything.

Georgian jewelry (which is seen much more rarely today than Victorian) is always of high karat gold. Stones are foiled, with closed, engraved backs.

Beautiful pastes (glass stones, cut as skillfully as real ones) were often used, and settings were minimized; the settings were crafted to show off the stones, rather than the opposite.

Art Nouveau has a very special look, with curved lines, graceful natural-istic forms, romantic ladies, flowers, leaves, trees. Since there are so many "repros" of Art Nouveau around, *always* ask carefully about any Art Nouveau piece, study it with *special attention,* and if you have any doubt at all, *pay no more* than a "repro" price for it!

Materials like bog oak, jet (*real* jet, not glass), gutta-percha (a hard brownish-black composition), and pieces of hair jewelry are rare now and virtually unreproduceable. Some, like gutta-percha, I have never seen in a contemporary piece—so if you find it, it's *old.*

Of course, you may have the luck to find a *dated* piece, and although even a date can be phonied, if everything else tallies, more than likely you have found the genuine article.

Now ask yourself:
4. Is it good of its kind?
Is it handmade, or machined? This is something you generally can tell. Look at the work through your loupe. If it is done by hand there will be irregulari-ties: if it is carved, you will be able to see the marks of the tool; if it is hand engraved, the pattern will vary slightly. The hand is never as precise as a machine, thank goodness!

Is the work on your piece delicate, careful, and loving—or careless and imitative? Again, if you study your finds, you can tell detailed, careful, individu-alistic work from work that says: "Fifty more like me were made today."

Are the proportions pleasing, the stones and settings well chosen? If *big-ness* is a virtue (like long ambers or jets), is this bigger, longer, better than most? If *smallness* is what you're looking for (delicate carving, filigree work, fine mosaic), is this superior in its fineness? Taste is not so intangible, when you begin to know the questions to ask.

To illustrate this point, I chose a modest example, well within the reach of most budgets, yet very much worth owning. The two "ivory" pins (see Illustration 6) look very much alike, yet one sold for $9 and the other for $21. The $21 pin was a bargain I bought eagerly; the $9 one I bought to show you what the difference is.

On the pin at right the ivory markings are clear. The material is "fatty" and shiny, with soft graining showing. The carving is delicate and very de-tailed; look at the rose! The hand is dainty, and even the fingernails are done with real art. When you turn the piece over, you see that the hinge, pin, and catch are of gold, well set into the ivory, and perfect. No part of the piece has ever been repaired or replaced. All in all, this is a perfect, elegant piece of its kind.

The pin at left is duller and shows no graining; its texture is coarse and "thinner." It is almost certainly made of bone. The carving of the hand and flower is much cruder and much less detailed; and a piece of the flower leaf, the very tip end, is missing. On the back is a difference, too; hinge, pin, and catch are made of brass, and there is a little gouge that might mean some work or repair was done once upon a time.

5. The final question, and the one only you can answer, is also the most important in terms of the decision to buy: **Do you love it? Is it beautiful to you? Do you really want to own it?**

I make it a rule of thumb to inspect everything interesting because I'm "addicted." But I *buy* only what I feel I "can't live without." When in doubt, I walk away and ask myself how I'd feel if I came back in half an hour and somebody else had made off with my find. If my stomach bunches, and I can't stand to think about it, back I go.

Believe it or not, it should not take you more than ten minutes (once you have developed a little technique) to ask these first five questions. The second five (the ones that may finally determine whether you *buy* or *pass by*) are a little subtler but just as specific. So read on!

6. Bone hand (left) and ivory hand

Chapter Five

The Next Five Questions to Ask

Unless you are a dealer and can resell anything you buy if you regret it later, making an antique jewelry purchase—even a small one—involves a pretty momentous decision. Nobody, no matter how wealthy, can afford to buy everything he or she likes—or even everything that passes the five-question test in the preceding chapter. As you gain expertise in your hunt for old jewelry, more and more tempting "buys" will come your way. Where do you stop? How do you decide what is truly worth owning, truly right for you, and what falls short? How do you save yourself from being inundated in jewelry, owning boxes and boxes of it, renting vault after vault to hold it, paying more insurance money than you can afford to cover it, inventing more and more wily plots to protect it? (I have one friend who hides her jewelry around the house and then truly "loses" it; sometimes—but not always—she manages to "find" what she wants when she wants it. But in these days of high crime rates and even higher insurance premiums, jewelry can become a burden rather than a pleasure if you let your buying power run away with you.)

In fact, it does not take an enormous amount of money to build a collection too unwieldy to handle, too big to enjoy. A few years of indiscriminate collecting, even on a very modest scale, can do it. And worse, by being too eager to buy, you can end up with a lot of "compromise" jewelry that you do not really want or enjoy wearing—a chipped mosaic pin rather like the fine one you felt you could not afford; a fake Wedgwood pendant that reminded you of something when you bought it, but doesn't now; a ring with pasted-in stones that you can wear only when you don't wash your hands; a necklace that doesn't go with anything; earrings that break every time you put them on; an unbecoming brooch that looked absolutely wonderful on somebody else.

The purpose of this chapter, then, is to pose some down-to-earth hard-facts questions that you should ask yourself, and answer wisely, *before* making a purchase. If you do, you will build a collection of old jewelry worth owning, worth wearing, and worth passing on to your children. It will give you pleasure in the buying, pleasure in all the years you own it, and will increase in value for as long as you hold it. You will never regret a single piece you purchase, and you will *not* make mistakes. Isn't that a goal worth striving for?

So let us assume that you have found a piece that passes the First Five Questions test. What is the next question to ask?

1. Is the piece wearable?

Many wonderful old pieces are not—and you may want them anyway. But for me, a book is to be read, an apple is to be eaten, and jewelry is to be worn. A magnificently fragile Lalique bracelet, no matter how glorious, could not give me the same pleasure as a fine, heavy, beautifully worked gold bangle with years of wear in it. The Lalique would live in the vault; the bangle would live on my wrist—as it was intended to. This reflects my philosophy of collecting; it may not be yours. To me, a piece that is too delicate for normal—even occasional—wear is a doubtful asset and usually (if I can) I pass it by. This goes for rings that are too unwieldy or delicate for comfortable wear (or have pasted stones, which would only end up giving me grief), for *most* foiled and hair rings because they have to be removed whenever you wash (although I confess to owning a few of these that I would not give up for anything, and cheerfully—and carefully—remove when necessary), and for rings with prongs or protuberances that catch on your clothes. Pins with insecure backs are a doubtful purchase too, unless you are absolutely sure (and you almost never can be) that a small repair or the addition of a "clutch" will secure them. Magnificent, heavy belt buckles that you will never wear are a questionable purchase too. The same goes for elaborate long earrings—popular with the Victorians, but out of place today on all but the most elegant occasions. If you have enough of those occasions, such earrings are fine for you; if your everyday life doesn't include them, the earrings may spend their whole life in your vault—an ignominious fate for something that was meant to give pleasure.

Today's fashions, fabrics, colors, and styles are different from yesterday's, and much jewelry intended to complement a specific fashion simply does not "go" today. You may love a heavy, carved jet chain and mourning locket—but will you wear it? If the answer is no, think twice about buying it. The delicate, almost insignificant little pins and lavalieres of the early twentieth century looked wonderful with the filmy fabrics and romantic fashions of pre-World War I—but they can get lost on today's bolder clothing. Ancient jewelry—high karat Greek and Roman gold, Egyptian beads, and the like— is often so delicate, and sometimes so costly—that you would not dare subject it to wear. You may still choose to buy such things—but be realistic: Wouldn't a handsome, 18-karat-or-lower piece that you could wear without worry suit you better? (I have Roman earrings that have never been out of the vault. They were not that expensive, and I love the thought that I own them—but I will never wear them. Ancient gold is unalloyed, as near to 24 karat as gold naturally occurs; it is so soft and delicate you could bend it with your finger. I look at them wistfully sometimes, but the earrings will stay forever in the vault.)

Stickpins are popular items of antique jewelry, and dealers sell a great many of them. Where do they go? Almost nobody wears them. Men complain they are so heavy that they make holes in ties; women find them insignificant alone, and a bother to put on and take off (each one with its own individual clutch—a *must!*) in twos and threes. And so they stay in a stickpin holder, or worse, in a box in the drawer, or still worse, they are "clipped," set into a tasteless little gold vase, and worn as bastardized "old" jewelry. They are expensive, often exquisite and appealing, but not very wearable; in recent years I have learned to sigh and pass them by.

Old watches can be a terrible problem. They are as crotchety as their age suggests and as hard to repair as anything I can think of. The swinging watch chains our grandmothers wore were either pinned to their bosoms or secured at their waists; we wear them hanging from our throats *(heavily)*, and bumping against (and denting) tables, countertops, and desks. If you are past forty, you may have trouble reading the time at the length of a doubled watch chain. And if you have a key-wind, you will probably, at some time in your life, lose or misplace the key. I love old watches, but I don't buy them anymore. They are too chancy, and I am too farsighted.

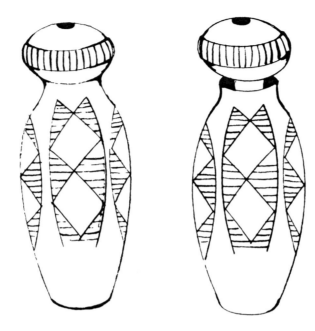

7. **A clutch (closed and partly open)**

Some pieces need a certain amount of care to keep them in their best condition. Watches need to be wound now and then. Opals should be soaked in water or glycerine from time to time. Ivory tends to react to moisture and so should be kept in an evenly heated room, not too dry and not too damp. (An ivory portrait is a poor investment for someone who lives at the seashore.) Amber is best kept away from light and air, as it may very gradually change color and tend to "crackle" when it is exposed. Pearls should not be kept in plastic, and should be worn and allowed to "breathe" with fair frequency; strands of pearls should be cleaned and reknotted by an expert when they begin to show soil. Turquoise picks up dirt and grease from its environment (from you, dirty dishwater, garden digging, anything) and will discolor if you don't protect it.

None of these "cautions" involves very much time or effort, but if you have a collection of jewelry with different crotchets and different needs, you must accommodate these if the pieces are to wear well. Therefore, when you add a new piece to your collection, it is reasonable to ask yourself: How much care will this piece need, and am I willing and able to give it? I never, never, buy seed pearls, though I love them, because I know that they are practically impossible to restring. They have to be treated with extreme care because they often are still strung on their original horsehair, and over the years it has dried out and grown fragile. If the hair breaks, jeweler after jeweler will groan over the difficulty of restringing them. The holes in the pearls are so tiny that almost nobody will take on the job, and if someone does it will be handwork—and very expensive. (The same is true of some branch coral.) If you do buy seed pearls, I strongly advise you to ask the dealer who is selling them to guarantee a repair (at your expense, of course) should you need it. If the dealer just smiles sadly and refuses, beware: she *can't* have them repaired—and probably you can't either.

Of course there are exceptions—and many of them—to what I have told you. But there are also many unhappy jewelry lovers who have fallen in love with a wonderful old piece, bought it eagerly, and never been able to enjoy it to the fullest. Before you buy, ask yourself: *Is it wearable?*—and answer with hard practicality. If the answer is *Not really,* or *Only after extensive* [or value-destroying] *repair,* or *Only for a little while*—think twice before you spend your money. If the answer is *No, but it is so beautiful, so full of history and human experience, so rare and special, that I can't pass it up*—buy it (you will, anyway), put it in the vault (as I did my Roman earrings), and visit it from time to time to renew your spirits.

But suppose that the piece you have your eye on has passed the wearability test, what is the next question to ask?

2. Is it right for me?

Jewelry is a very personal possession, perhaps the most personal, and it is meant to enhance your appearance. It seems ridiculously obvious to say so, but before you buy any piece of jewelry, new or old, you certainly should try it on and make sure that it becomes *you* Some people find gold unbecoming; others don't like silver. Massive pieces (like those from the mid-Victorian period) are too heavy and clumsy for delicately built, small women, and slim, fragile Edwardian pieces are too "insignificant" for women built on a more Junoesque scale. A long thin face can be accentuated by long, busy earrings, and a short, thick neck can look like no neck at all in a heavy choker. I can't wear topazes, much as I admire them on the shelf (and on other people); the color is all wrong for me. And beautiful old garnet pins, which I enjoy looking at, are wrong for me, too, so there is no point in buying them. In short, *scale, style, and color* of jewelry must be taken into account when you ask yourself: Is this piece right for me?

Old style and costume books are full of advice on what kind of jewelry to wear in order to enhance one's natural attributes. We wear so much more makeup (and are so much more aware of the possibilities of altering our appearance with cosmetics) than our grandmothers that we don't seem to give as much thought as they did to the benefits we can get from jewelry. Heavy bangle bracelets, for example, tend to make a large hand look smaller; handsome rings call attention to the hand; sparkling stones—diamonds are the prime example—make the eyes sparkle and seem larger; stones at the ears that complement the color of the eyes make them seem deeper in color; dark jewelry, like jet, garnets, dark ambers, or tortoise, set off and complement pale skin. You will observe yourself that long heavy chains and massive pins tend to make short stout women look dumpy; large rings make short, fat fingers look shorter and fatter; long earrings and short necks simply do not go together.

There is no great trick to knowing what looks good on you in jewelry: the problem is simply that we tend not to think about that when we are really "smitten" with a piece. But in order to get the pleasure—and the adornment value—from your jewelry, you should make sure that it is as becoming in color, proportion, and "fit" as a dress or a pair of shoes.

As you collect more jewelry, you will be aware that certain pieces go with each other. Buy with an eye to what you can wear with what. If you want to buy a chain, try to carry with you the locket you plan to hang on it; the colors of the gold may be different, the proportions may be wrong, the length may not be suitable. Dealers in antique jewelry are on the whole less accommodating than other merchants about taking things back if you change your mind. Therefore, it is important that you think carefully about each purchase, try it on, check it out, and make sure that it is right for you, and serves its purpose— makes you look, and feel, more beautiful—*before* you decide to buy.

3. Does it advance my collection?

There is a philosophy to collecting *anything* that applies equally well to collecting antique jewelry: buy only what you truly like and want to live with for a long time; try to specialize in your collecting, since a collection that centers on *something* specific is of more interest (and dollar value) than a random sampling of objects; value the special and perfect (no matter how modest) above the shoddy and careless (no matter how expensive); try always to "trade up"—exchange the lesser piece for a better one, when you find it.

How does this apply to antique jewelry? As you begin to accumulate a few pieces—and to know where your taste (and pocketbook) can lead you— think of the pieces you own as a *collection*, and add to them thoughtfully and wisely. Perhaps you are especially fond of rings. When you add a new one, think of how it will combine with the ones you already have. Antique rings look well in combinations, even two and three rings to a finger, if they "live well" with each other. I have seen a hand of rings in rubies and rose diamonds, each ring complementing and "setting off" the others, that was magnificent. Each one was obviously chosen with care to "live with" its neighbors. Small pieces of jewelry especially—stickpins, small memorial pins, lace pins—can be bought inexpensively and may be insignificant alone, but in combination can be stunning and unique. The same is true for chains: a group of three, perhaps, each a bit longer than its neighbor, can be far more dramatic than one chain alone. A long old silver link chain and the very same pattern of chain in gold, worn together, are rich and beautiful; each enhances the other and bespeaks the owner's daring and taste.

I bought a single baby ring some years ago because it was lovely and inexpensive; now I have perhaps forty (probably more as you read this; I can't resist them!)—and each one different and enchanting. I wear them in combinations hung on an antique baby bracelet and hooked by a massive watch swivel to a chain. They never fail to excite other collectors; in fact, I feel sometimes as if I have "made" the market for baby rings, which are no longer inexpensive at all! Collections of things are worth more than the value of the individual pieces, as *pairs* of things are worth more than double the price of a single piece, and *sets* of things are worth more than the value of each piece alone. As you buy jewelry, try to see the possibilities of specialized collecting, look for "pairing" or "matching" pieces, or pieces that go well in combination with one another. If you are careful and not reckless in your buying, as you accumulate pieces they will reflect your unique taste and intelligence, will live well with each other, and will truly be a "collection," not just a grab bag of impulse purchases that bear no relationship to one another.

Some collectors specialize in a period—Art Nouveau, perhaps, or Edwardian jewelry, or Georgian pieces; some in a country—French, or English, or Russian, or American pieces; some in a category of jewelry—memorial pieces, or watch chains, or mosaic brooches, or even baby rings! Many collectors specialize in more than one area, and almost all serious antique jewelry buyers are ready to expand into a different direction if a really fabulous piece comes along. But having a sense of the "profile" of your collection—what you have and what you are looking for—makes your collecting more valuable and more fun. Besides, when you're browsing it's always more impressive to be able to tell a curious dealer, "I'm looking for a super baby ring" than to say, "I'm just looking."

As for "trading up"—as you become more sophisticated in your collecting, you may find that some of the pieces you bought earlier no longer fit in with your collection, or simply are not being worn because you have found pieces similar—and better—that you prefer. You can choose to keep these early pieces anyway (old jewelry never really is outgrown), to give them as gifts to deserving and beloved friends or relatives (thus starting them off on a collecting adventure of their own), or to "trade them in" on pieces that now suit you better.

In these times, when good antique jewelry is fairly hard to come by, most dealers will eagerly accept your invitation to sell or trade old jewelry. Of course they are in business for profit, and you cannot expect them to offer you a retail price, but if you have held the pieces long enough in today's rising market, it is perfectly possible to actually make a profit on the trade or sale and still leave the dealer room to make a profit too. Usually a dealer will trade only when you are buying something more expensive than what you are trading, and so some cash will be changing hands. But a dealer will nearly always buy if your jewelry is good. It will also be an instructive experience for you to watch the dealer evaluate your pieces, asking in her head the same questions you do, and determining *in seconds* what your jewelry is worth at this moment, in this transaction.

4. Is it a good buy?

Are you surprised to see this question so far down on the list? No piece is a good buy, at any price, if you have not determined that it is really worth buying. Providing that you have, though, how do you decide whether the price the dealer asks for it is fair, excessive, or a bargain?

Perhaps the best way—and the dealers' own way—is by comparison shopping. Dealers set their prices by 1) what they paid for a piece, 2) what the current market value is, and sometimes, regrettably, 3) what the traffic will bear. Dealers who do not mark their prices, or who mark them in code only, are often using the unfair third criterion as a guideline in setting price. You should be aware of this; curiously, it may work for you as well as against you—as many dealers will give a favorable price to someone they want to sell to as often as they will give a stiff one to someone they don't like or who they think is rich enough to pay the difference. If a price is clearly marked, however (even though it may be elastic, or negotiable), you can determine whether a piece is within your range before you begin actually to talk about how many dollars it costs.

In a general sort of way, there are relationships between pieces that can help you to approximate a fair price. For example, a fine heavy chain in 18 karat gold may sell for as much as $400. In sterling silver, a chain of comparable quality might be about $80—or one-fifth that amount. In gold filled, a chain of comparable quality might cost perhaps $50, or one-eighth the price.

These relationships are only approximations—guidelines, rather than stable pricing guides. And the rapid changes in retail prices; the price differential between sections of the country (on the whole, prices in the East are lower than prices in the West, and prices in small towns are lower than prices in big cities); the fact that when you are willing to buy more than one piece, prices are more readily adjustable than when you want to buy one piece only; plus all of the variables that depend on the dealer's investment, overhead, eagerness to sell, and the length of time the piece has been held—all these, and more, enter into pricing.

Nevertheless we can say that, in general, if a piece is offered to you below what comparable pieces are selling for, or if it is offered at the same price as similar pieces but is more desirable in some way, and if you want it, it is a good buy. Incidentally, don't be misled by a dealer's willingness to come down in price from the amount originally quoted. Many dealers expect to do this, and have priced their things accordingly, but it is only common sense that the price you ultimately agree upon will be close to or exactly (or perhaps even above) the price the dealer knew in advance she would be willing to sell for. Some dealers may not negotiate at all; some may end up offering you a piece at half price. This does not in any way indicate whether or not the piece is a good buy. I would, in fact, buy more comfortably from the dealer who, on the first offer, quoted me a firm and fair price—but that is not everybody's preference. It is the *final* agreed-upon price that should be at or below fair market value if you are getting a good buy.

And if the piece is wonderful, and your buy is fair and reasonable though not a bargain, all other things being equal, buy it anyway. You are now close enough to perfection not to quibble over a small monetary difference (an amount you might squander anyway) on a piece that you will remember, and hunt vainly for, forever after.

So, providing the price is right, and everything else is right too, what else is there to ask?

5. Will it increase in value?

Almost any piece of antique jewelry in today's rising market can—if it has passed all the previous tests—be expected to increase in value; of course, some pieces stand a better chance than others. This question, as you see, is low on the list for most buyers, but it is important. It should be considered so that you will not be faced with disappointments if you should want or need to turn some of your collection back to cash.

In general, the cost of bread and the cost of gold have been fairly constant in their relationship since the sixteenth century! A University of California study last year proved that an ounce of gold today buys as much bread as it did in 1560, and that through the ages its value has varied less than one percent relative to the price of other commodities. This means that, although the price of your jewelry may rise as you hold it, unless it outstrips the general inflation and the price of gold, the rise is illusory, and the piece is not—in purely financial terms—a "good investment."

In recent years, however, antiques of all kinds and particularly portable antiques—things easily transported from country to country or easily stored in vaults—have increased in value beyond this general inflationary rise. The knowledge that they have moved so far so fast has made them doubly desirable, thereby increasing their upward price spiral. Notice, please, that this means they are more expensive to *buy*, as well as more lucrative to *sell*, and therefore when you buy antique jewelry for investment, you are gambling that the price will continue to go up at the same, or a similar, rate.

The really sage investor does not buy what everybody else wants; instead, he or she looks for *tomorrow's* good investment. And so it is with antique jewelry: if you are buying with an eye to investment, you should, in general, stay away from what is in vogue today, and look instead for what might be in vogue tomorrow.

Art Nouveau and Art Deco are both enjoying a tremendous vogue as of this writing. Prices are high and, concomitantly, reproduction is rampant. In general, you will not get a "good buy" in these areas—though you may buy marvelous pieces well worth their price to you. It is in the nature of vogues that they play themselves out; therefore, Art Nouveau and Art Deco will, in all likelihood, not be as popular—or as high-priced—in a few years as they are today. Hence, they are not, in purely monetary terms, a "good investment."

What is not popular today that may be tomorrow? At the moment *lavalieres and brooches* generally enjoy less of a vogue than *chains and rings;* dealers find them harder to sell, and the prices reflect this. If you don't believe it, look at any ring and any pin priced at $100 in the same dealer's display case. Compare the workmanship, size of the stones, condition, weight, and karat of gold. Chances are, there will be more to look at in the pin—but the ring will sell faster. Old rings are at a premium, and so are higher in price. The pin is probably a better "investment."

Hair jewelry has just begun to take off in popularity, but I am sure there are still places where it can be bought for very little money. In the big cities of the East, a fine hair chain with gold findings may sell for $50 to $75. I have bought them in country flea markets for as little as $4. (Note that if I did not like and wear them, I would not have bought them at all!) One was even given to me free (with a "yuch!" from the dealer, who hated hair), as a bonus for buying the gold filled watch hook attached to it. If hair jewelry is your passion, and you can still buy it cheaply, it is probably a good investment, destined to increase in value.

In general, any material made in the nineteenth century (or earlier) that is *not* being made today will probably go the same way as hair jewelry. Gutta-percha (described earlier) will, I think, go sky-high in price within a few years. *If* you like it and can find it cheaply, I'd stock up on it today. The same is true of gunmetal, bog oak, jet, and genuine old cut steel. (Marcasite, which looks similar to cut steel, is already vogue-y as part of Art Deco, and already widely reproduced.) I love, and still buy, inexpensive tortoise piqué when I can find it, but it is becoming increasingly rare and has skyrocketed in price. Turn-of-the-century English silver sentimental pins with names, mizpah, or doves-and-hearts-and-flowers designs on them are still easy to find and relatively inexpensive; I have recently paid $14 to $24 for them. All silver is going up, and will continue to go up as long as gold rises. (The price of gemstones, too, follows the price of gold.) Glass beads have already seen a tremendous rise in price; what you could buy for $2 or $3 a few years ago now sells for ten times that much, or more. But you may still find good buys in glass beads *if* you know the old ones from new reproductions.

Of course, what I have said here does not apply *unless* the piece in question also has passed all the tests for condition, age, and fineness. A poor piece, of any kind, will never gain in value at all.

As for less modest pieces—I feel that Georgian jewelry, already high-priced, is becoming scarce enough so that a good piece, priced reasonably, is a good investment—better perhaps than a piece of a later period with the same quality and price. Goldwork, I think, will increase in value faster than gemstones will; that is, I would prefer to *invest* in a fine Castellani or Fabergé piece (a signed piece is *always* good if the signature is a famous one!) than in a fine diamond—if rising value were my main consideration.

But I must repeat my warning: I do *not* mean to suggest that you should buy antique jewelry as a hedge against inflation. In fact, I am sad about this practice; beautiful jewelry should be bought to be loved and worn—as any art should be enjoyed as a life-enhancing, rather than a financial, asset. However, when you are buying, it is reasonable to ask yourself: Will this increase in value?—and to know the answer as well as you can, and consider it in making your purchase.

All the ten important questions I have suggested can be considered in minutes once you have gained some expertise. It is rare indeed that one piece will rate "perfect" on all of them. If the piece you choose comes close, and you can afford it, buy it and enjoy it with much pleasure. And if it doesn't, and you love it anyway and can afford it, buy it and good luck to you. For it is *love* and not money that makes collectors, ultimately. All the sensible considerations can be wrong if love and enjoyment of the piece are not present. That is the cardinal rule of life, and art.

What You'll Be Looking At: Metals

Part of the fascination of old jewelry is that no matter how much you look at, you will always see something different. Each piece is unique, has a personality all its own, and embodies its own mysteries: What is it made of, where did it come from and when, who made it, who wore it and loved it, did it have a special function or meaning or "magic," what "family" of jewelry does it belong to, and in what way is it unique or special?

Some of these questions can never be answered, but many of them can. And the more you know about your jewelry, the more personal it is to you, the more interesting it is to own and wear.

We have already mentioned some of the materials old jewelry is made of and how to recognize them. Now let's talk a bit about the *precious metals*—gold, silver, and platinum—how to identify them, read their marks, and understand their "personalities."

Gold has been treasured since ancient times as the ideal metal for jewelry. Its rarity makes it desirable, its color is rich and becoming, it is soft enough to work easily, and in its pure state it will never tarnish. When gold implements from ancient times are unearthed, they are as bright and new looking as the day they left their maker's hand. Gold can be beaten into tissue-paper thinness or drawn out into wire of hairlike fineness (an ounce of gold can be drawn out into fifty miles of wire!). It is heavier than lead and gives a satisfying feeling of solidity and "fatness" in the hand. When gold is alloyed with various other metals, it can give a wide range of beautiful colors. The alloying also increases the wearing qualities of the gold, which is important when it is used in jewelry (like rings and chains) that will be worn a long time and must be able to withstand a certain amount of banging and abrasion.

Pure gold is called *24 karat* (although absolutely pure gold almost never occurs naturally; a museum curator told me that he once identified a faked gold antiquity because the gold in it was "too pure.") Gold marked 18 karats (in England it is spelled "carats"; therefore *18c* or *18ct.* would mark a piece as English) should be at least 18 parts of gold to 6 of alloy. In practice, however, suppliers can sell gold that varies ½ karat from what it is marked; therefore, an 18k piece may actually be as little as 17½k. Although the gold content is far from the most important factor about antique jewelry (many dealers will act offended if you are too interested in it, and will remind you that they are not selling gold bullion, but art), the price they have paid has probably varied in proportion to the gold content, and so will the price you pay; thus, you certainly should know as much as you can about it.

In England before 1854, "gold" meant high karat gold—18 karat or better. In that year 15, 12, and 9 karat gold were legally recognized, and—in 1932—14 karat gold replaced 12 and 15 karat. Therefore, the gold content of English jewelry can be a help in dating it. Georgian jewelry, by definition, *must* be 18 karat gold or better. I have been offered "Georgian" chains stamped 9ct—but Victoria had been on the throne almost twenty years when 9 karat gold was legalized!

Most, but not all, English gold jewelry is stamped with marks indicating the city where it was assayed, the karat of gold, a date letter for the year it was stamped, and perhaps even the maker. If you love old jewelry, it is worth buying a book that lists all these marks (the gold and silver marks are substantially the same, and the book will enable you to read both). It does take a little practice to read the date marks, but making the effort is well worth your while. The karat mark, however, is easily read; it is usually expressed in this form: "15 .625," "14 .585," and so on. From 1784 most English gold and silver was marked with the head of the reigning sovereign, but in 1890 this mark was abolished, and so English marked pieces *with* the sovereign's head would be dated *before 1890.* Very early English gold and silver was marked with a crowned lion's head facing forward; in 1821 the head was turned in profile and the crown was removed. After 1844 the "lion passant" (in profile) was used only as a mark for sterling silver. So if you find a gold piece with the lion passant or, even more exciting, with the crowned lion facing forward, you have a clue as to its age as well as its country of origin.

The French mark you will most often see is a tiny eagle's head—so small, in fact, that without inspecting it with a loupe you may take it for a nick in the gold. It is usually placed on the outside of the piece, but often you have to look hard for it. If you find it, it means the piece was not only made in France, but is 18 karat gold or better, as in France it is illegal to sell as "gold" anything with a lower gold content.

A few words more about the karat. Although high karat gold is desirable because of its value and the malleability with which it can be worked, it has its drawbacks, too. It is extremely heavy (which can be a problem in large brooches or long chains), and it is soft and easily dented, scratched, and nicked. Humbler low karat gold will wear better and needs less care—especially important when you're buying rings and bracelets, which take a lot of punishment. I'm sure you have all seen high karat gold wedding rings worn to dangerous thinness; you will probably never see a 9 karat ring in that condition. High karat chains, too, tend to wear and consequently break and perhaps get lost, and high karat rings with set stones tend to lose their stones more easily than their low karat counterparts. This is not to be taken as an argument against high karat gold jewelry; it is simply a fact you should be aware of in buying and taking care of whatever gold jewelry you own and cherish.

Gold can be worked in a variety of ways, nearly all of them dating as far back as the history of gold itself. From earliest times, gold has been beaten or hammered; decorated with chasing (hammering from the front with punches), repoussé (hammering from the back into two- or even three-dimensional forms), engraving (incising lines, dots, or patterns from the front with sharp tools), or stamping (using punching tools with patterns that could be repeated over and over).

Since the third millennium before Christ, gold wire has been used for filigree (woven or twined threads of metal) work, and for rings and chains. Gold ("hard") soldering was known from about this time, and only a little later "granulation" (hard soldering of tiny grains of gold to a gold surface), which was so admired and earnestly copied by the Victorians, was perfected by Etruscan goldsmiths.

Casting of precious metals was not used much by the ancients, but they did know about, and occasionally use, the lost wax process. By this method a model is made in wax, surrounded by a mold, and then heated. The wax runs out and is lost, and molten metal is poured into the mold to take its place. When the metal cools, the mold is broken off, and the piece is removed. We do not know exactly when lost wax casting was invented, but we do know it was used by the ancient Egyptians.

Many lovers of antique jewelry believe that if a piece is cast, it cannot be old; obviously this is not true. But if a piece is crudely *machine* cast in a process repeated over and over, it clearly must date from the use of machines for jewelry work—probably no earlier than the middle of the nineteenth century, and perhaps much later.

The most famous and elusive imitation gold ever made was *pinchbeck,* an alloy of copper and zinc developed in eighteenth-century London by a Fleet Street watchmaker, Christopher Pinchbeck. Real pinchbeck, made during the lifetime of Christopher or his son, to whom he passed his secret formula, looked like gold and wore like gold, without tarnishing. But the secret was lost with the Pinchbecks, and no one has been able to duplicate it since. Many dealers will eagerly offer any kind of yellow metal jewelry *except* gold as "pinchbeck," even if it was made yesterday. But you should remember that the term "pinchbeck" is as specific as the term "gold"—and should not be used carelessly. All *real* pinchbeck jewelry dates back to the eighteenth century.

We have already discussed the ways of distinguishing gold jewelry from gold filled by studying it through the loupe. Real experts can "weigh" gold in their hand and recognize it by its weight—sometimes even to the karat! The most reliable procedure, however—for experts and amateurs alike—is to test it by using a touchstone, nitric acid, and standard gold needles. The touchstone and needles (and the bottles to hold the acid) can be bought at a jewelry supply store. The acid must be purchased separately. The process is this: firmly rub the gold object (preferably in a place that will not be spoiled by the friction) onto the touchstone so that it leaves a clear mark. Rub the appropriate needles (which are marked as to their karat, 10, 12, 14, and the like) on the stone near your original mark. Then, using the bottle stopper, draw a wet line of nitric acid across the marks and watch them through a magnifying glass. The mark of the needle that acts most like the mark of the object you're testing will identify the karat. Low karat gold will disappear almost immediately; 14 karat gold will linger a moment, then "tarnish" and disappear; 18 karat gold or higher will not disappear completely, but will leave a bloom of gold on the stone after you wipe off the acid.

Heavy gold filled or rolled gold jewelry will "test" the same as real gold, since what you are rubbing onto the touchstone *is* real gold. Therefore, you must look at a piece carefully and make sure no gold is worn off to disclose base metal underneath. Many jewelers and dealers will file a gold piece to make sure that it is gold throughout, and then drop acid on the filed portion. If it turns green: brass; if not, gold. I find filing a barbaric practice that spoils many a beautiful piece. I would rather be uncertain whether or not a piece is gold, and preserve its beauty intact, than file it and be sure. Filing to me is like throwing out the baby with the bathwater, but that is a personal philosophy; if you absolutely must know whether a piece is solid gold or not, filing may be the only choice.

Gold needs little care, aside from the normal common sense procedures. It should not be dropped or scraped or cleaned with an abrasive that will scratch it. The easiest way to clean it is to lower the piece gently (unless water or soap will damage it) into a small glassful of detergent or shampoo solution, let it stand for a few minutes, and then rinse it off and wipe it dry. For stubborn dirt, adding ammonia to the water and brushing with a small brush (an eyebrow brush is perfect) should do the trick. A rouge cloth or polishing cloth, sold in jewelry supply stores, will make gold pieces shine; but sometimes antique pieces look better when they don't shine—their soft patina is more beautiful than a glossy "new" look. Most jewelry stores and all jewelry supply houses sell a solution for cleaning—usually a pink liquid in a jar in which you can immerse metal jewelry for a few minutes, then rinse it off. This works very well for gold jewelry, but no better, really, than a simple detergent-ammonia solution you can put together yourself. Be very careful not to drop your jewelry roughly into a solution; also, check for loose stones, and to make sure there are no pearls, opals, hair, amber, ivory, or any other materials on the piece that would be damaged by water or acids, *before* you dip. Make sure, too, that there are no pasted-in stones (usually the glue is clearly seen if you examine through a loupe) because they will come out in the soaking. When you rinse, never hold the pieces under running water in an open sink; too many stones have disappeared that way. Instead, close the sink, rinse gently in clear water over a basin or bowl, and then check each piece carefully before you pour the rinse water out. For diamond pieces, extra sparkle is added if you give them a bath in regular rubbing alcohol before drying them off. Again, it is best to dry them with a soft cloth, not with a loopy towel that may catch in the prongs or pull hinges or pins out of place. Gentleness is the keynote! For really dirty gold jewelry, a bath in straight ammonia may be the answer, followed by a scrubbing with your eyebrow brush and a little soap or baking soda. Always use the *least* amount of cleaning necessary to get results, and scrub, handle, push, and pull as *little* as possible.

Silver has been used for jewelry at least as long as gold, perhaps longer, since it occurs more commonly in nature. It weighs only about half as much as gold, and is not as malleable and easy to work (an ounce of silver can be drawn into a mile of wire). It is much cheaper than gold, has greater reflective power, and is resistant to many chemicals. However, it does tarnish in the presence of sulfur—a much greater problem today than it was before the industrial revolution, when the air was relatively pure.

Like gold, silver is too soft in its natural form to be useful for jewelry; it has to be alloyed with a harder metal, almost always copper. The best known combination is "sterling silver": 92 parts per thousand of copper to 908 of silver. In England the proportions for "sterling" are 75 parts of copper to 925 of silver. For "Britannia" standard (not the same as britannia metal), which is less frequently seen, the proportions are 958.4 parts of silver per thousand. "Fine" silver means pure silver. "Coin silver" means 900 parts per thousand of silver to 100 of copper. "Silver" or "Solid Silver" mean the same as "Sterling Silver."

Silver jewelry made in other countries, especially African and East European silver, may vary greatly in actual silver content.

Silver has not been as universally popular for jewelry as gold, probably because it is not as rare and therefore not as expensive. It has always been used for peasant jewelry and often for costume jewelry. During the 1870s it enjoyed a huge spurt in popularity. In England, Queen Victoria, coming out of deepest mourning, approved wearing silver at court. She liked Scotch agate jewelry, most often set in silver, and the preference of this dumpy, unattractive lady influenced fashions profoundly—silver was suddenly "in." Beautiful English chains and lockets and bracelets and brooches from this period are plentiful and often very elegant. By the 1880s, however, silver was "out," though not for long. The Art Nouveau jewelers, seeking to find beauty in the humblest of materials, loved silver and used it extensively, in combination with semiprecious stones like agates, amethysts, baroque pearls, and so on. At the turn of the century it again enjoyed a great vogue, and in the 1920s and 1930s silver once again became a popular favorite for jewelry.

Silver had been used extensively since the eighteenth century to set diamonds because it has greater reflectivity and tended to make the diamonds look white, rather than yellowish, as gold does. A silver diamond setting on a gold ring or pin usually indicates an old piece. Toward the end of the nineteenth century, platinum replaced silver and gold as the most popular setting for diamonds.

The great and unique charm of silver is that as it gets older, it wears to a soft patina of considerable beauty. The pattern of scratches, far from being undesirable, gives it its special quality and is treasured. To have old silver repolished or lacquered would be ludicrous, and the rhodium plating of much modern silver (which keeps it from tarnishing, but also from wearing into this soft patina) is to my mind a ridiculous gilding of the lily. In the old days, the finest silver polishing material was thought to be the soft ash of a fine cigar. Nowadays, soaking in a detergent and ammonia solution (with the same cautions as apply to gold jewelry) or rubbing with a jeweler's rouge cloth or silver polishing cloth gives good results. Ordinary kitchen cream of tartar will do a lovely, soft job, very like what our grandmothers aimed for with cigar ash. The one material I do *not* like is pink cream or lotion silver polish; it seems to get in all the cracks in such a way that it is impossible to get out. Some silver jewelry has been "antiqued" or treated with chemicals that darken parts of the pattern; these cannot be cleaned out by ordinary polishing solutions. Niello (silver inlaid with bluish black enamellike material) cannot and should not be "rubbed off"; it is part of the body of the piece, not a painted on or chemicalized finish. Never use abrasives harsher than cream of tartar on your silver jewelry, or you may damage and scratch it irretrievably. If the tarnish really bothers you, a little hairspray will guard the surface a bit without making it shiny, as lacquers or wax would do. Do not use colorless nail polish; it will look ugly, and when you try to take it off, you may spoil the patina of your fine silver pieces.

It is not hard to recognize silver jewelry. Most of it is marked, and few other white metals were used in place of silver. Pewter was sometimes used, but rarely; it is much "grayer" looking than silver. Once in a while you may come upon a silver piece nielloed to look like gunmetal, and in that case testing with acid would be helpful. I have never seen either silver plated or Sheffield plated jewelry, though I have seen base metal jewelry that was "silver dipped"—a more recent procedure. If you are in doubt, choose a place on the jewelry that does not show, and touch a wee bit of nitric acid to it. If it is silver, the acid will turn *creamy*. Wipe it off immediately, or it will leave a "clean" stain that is hard to polish back to the original patina. If the acid turns green, your piece is brass or brass-alloyed metal.

Pieces marked "German silver" or "Nickel silver" have no silver at all in them. They are made of an alloy of copper, nickel, and zinc, popular as a silver substitute in the nineteenth century. German silver has a yellower tinge than silver and really looks different if you see the two together.

Tarnished silver has a characteristic smell, and if you rub old silver between your fingers until it warms up and sniff it, you can probably identify silver by this means alone. Try it; it's easier (and better for your jewelry) than using the acid test.

Although other metals have sometimes been used for jewelry, the only others that you will encounter with fair frequency in antique jewelry are gunmetal (an alloy of 9 parts copper to 1 part tin), cut steel, and—if you are lucky—Berlin iron. Cut steel jewelry has been popular since the eighteenth century. It was informal day jewelry, and probably originated as a cheaper alternative to marcasite. Marcasite is a real mineral, iron pyrites; it was very popular in the eighteenth century, too—set around the frames of lockets, cameos, and the like or worked in narrow bands to form patterned brooches. It was always set in silver, in beautifully rubbed-up mountings. As time went on, marcasite lost its glamour and became a cheap material used in cheap jewelry. It was still set in silver by the twentieth century, but was usually pasted in and used to give a sleazy glitter.

Cut steel, however, which aped marcasite in the eighteenth century, continued into the nineteenth and gained in stature. Each piece of steel was cut and faceted by hand, and hand riveted to the backing. One of the ways to tell cut steel from marcasite is to look for these rivets on the back. As cut steel grew in popularity, its purpose grew more ambitious, too: to imitate diamonds; the bits of steel were more intricately faceted and more beautifully set. In the late eighteenth century a large stud might have as many as 15 facets, and many of the pieces rivaled the finest diamond parures for intricacy and beauty. In the vaults of the New-York Historical Society there is a magnificent parure of cut steel proudly tagged: "Worn at the Lafayette Ball." Napoleon bought a cut steel parure for Marie Louise of Austria.

Chatelaines, buttons, buckles, necklaces, bracelets, and brooches of cut steel from this period are real finds. Often they are elaborately set onto two or three interlocking backings—sometimes with parts that turn or move. Rosettes, stars, or Greek key designs are typical of this period. Later cut steel pieces from the nineteenth century show the Victorians' interest in bugs, butterflies, lizards, bees, and the like. Toward the end of the nineteenth century, cut steel (like everything else) began to be cheaply manufactured and suffered a consequent decline in quality and popularity. By the end of the nineteenth century it was practically a lost craft.

Berlin iron jewelry is rare and hard to come by. It was delicately and beautifully cast during the War of Liberation against Napoleon (1813–15). Patriotic German ladies who turned in their gold jewelry to help the war effort were rewarded with black painted iron equivalents, often inscribed: *"Gold gab ich für Eisen"* ("I gave gold for iron"). The earlier iron jewelry aped popular gold jewelry of the day: parures of classical cameolike heads held together with fine chains; earrings and buckles and pins and bracelets of mesh or whorled iron wire, flower-patterned medallions and ornaments. Toward the middle of the century some Gothic-styled iron jewelry was made, but by 1850 the fad had passed, and the vogue for iron jewelry was over.

If you are lucky enough to find old Berlin iron jewelry, it will probably be surprisingly expensive. If it isn't, and you are sure of what you are buying, snap it up! Usually the only care that you will have to take of it is to be sure that it does not rust. If it does, a light wiping with kerosene or oil should take care of it, and a berth where there is not too much moisture in the air, plus a little oil now and then, should keep it in condition. If the black surface has worn or flecked off, you can safely touch it up with a bit of dull black paint.

Chapter Seven

What You'll Be Looking At:
Stones and Settings

Much can be learned about a piece by carefully studying the stones in it and how they were set, the pins and clasps, and the general shape and style. In looking at old jewelry you must remember, like a detective, that no one thing will tell you the whole story, but every detail can give you a clue, if you are skilled and patient enough to unravel it.

The way that stones are cut and set, though not conclusive in itself, can help in determining the age of a piece. Gemstones were not faceted at all until the Middle Ages. Before that they were polished as cabochons (with round, domed shapes) or used in their natural crystal forms. Early faceting was simple and flat; stones were valued for their color and "mystical qualities" rather than their brilliance. Diamonds, which we first find in Roman jewelry, occur in nature as eight-sided crystals. These crystals were popular during the seventeenth century in rings with which lovers wrote their names in the glass panes of windows. The earliest diamond cutters simply sliced off the top of the octahedron to make a flat "table."

By the sixteenth century the *rose cut,* a flat-bottomed faceted cut with a domed point on top, was developed, and the popularity of diamonds was assured. Rose diamonds, fondly called "roses," appear in jewelry for the next three centuries; they were particularly beloved by the Victorians. The rose cut was used on other stones, too, primarily the garnet, and rose cut garnets graced many a fine nineteenth-century piece.

Brilliant cutting of diamonds was developed around the beginning of the eighteenth century, and the principle of multifaceting stones to increase their showiness and brilliance was extended to the cutting of other gems. In fact, the eighteenth century was the age of gems, with goldwork and settings retreating in importance until they could scarcely be seen at all. Settings were made for gems, rather than gems being used to enhance or "point up" designs in gold and silver. The ingenuity of the eighteenth century also produced *paste*—a brilliant glass that was cut, faceted, and set with as much art and care as was lavished on gemstones. Pastes were not "imitation" stones at all; they were made in colors and shapes that could not be achieved with gemstones. To paraphrase a famous advertisement, they were not fake anything: they were "real paste."

Side View

8. Georgian ring

To enhance the color and brilliance of both stones and paste, *foils* were used—pieces of silver fitted into the backs of settings and painted or tinted to "assist" the stone. Naturally, to hold the foils, the settings had to be closed in back, and eighteenth-century settings are always closed this way, sometimes embellished with carving or enameling, so that the wrong side of the setting is as beautiful and carefully wrought as the right side. (See Illustration 8.) Over the years, moisture often penetrated into the backs of these old rings and tarnished or changed the color of the foils, and so many eighteenth-century diamond rings seem grayish, bluish, or greenish, and many foiled pastes and crystals show colors ranging from greens and blues to pinks and yellows that are different from their original appearance. Most pieces of this period were pavé set (stones lying smoothly side by side without metal showing), with stones of the same or closely matched colors, but with slightly varying sizes and cuts. The settings were handmade for the stones, and each one was a little bit different.

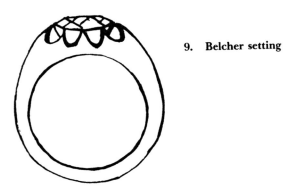

9.   **Belcher setting**

In the early nineteenth century, partly because of the rediscovery of the magnificent goldwork of the ancients, metalwork came into its own again, and settings assumed more importance. From Victoria's time onward, foiling lost popularity, settings were opened up in the back, and stones, instead of being held in collets (high collars of metal "rubbed up" over the stones), were more often enhanced in brilliance by being set in claws and prongs or held by beads of metal. Another popular style of setting in the late nineteenth century was the *"gypsy setting,"* where a small stone was set in a star-shaped depression, flat against the gold of the ring. When you see a stone set this way, it more or less dates the ring within a decade or two of the turn of the century. The same is true of the *"belcher setting,"* a heavy four-clawed setting in which a small stone is held in large heavy prongs that seem to encircle it like arms.

Bearing in mind that in many old pieces stones have been replaced and settings have been tampered with, you can still tell something about age from the style and cut of stones and settings. Certain cuts, certain settings, are characteristic of periods, and if they are "wrong," the piece may be wrong. As a very obvious example, antiquities should never have fully faceted stones. But you are more likely to encounter less blatant combinations. A Georgian ring should have a closed setting; a foiled stone should not show any marks on the setting (closed, up close to the stone) that indicate the stone has been replaced; pavé-set stones or pastes should be all of the same height in profile (though not necessarily of the same exact size or color). Victorians were very fond of little circular balls of moonstone, and these often appear in rings dating within a decade or so of the turn of the century. I have never seen them in a modern ring (unless they were put there to make it look "old"), nor in a ring earlier than, say, 1880.

The tremendous insistence on "blue-white" flawless brilliant-cut diamonds is fairly recent; often, in old rings and pins, beautiful rose-cut and old mine-cut (a transitional brilliant cut, with a wider table than today's more intricately faceted brilliant) diamonds were used that showed flaws or off colors. The Art Nouveau gold and silversmiths purposely *chose* flawed stones and featured them—baroque pearls, cloudy emeralds—as more interesting, more "natural," than "perfect" ones.

If diamonds are set in silver on an otherwise gold piece, the piece is usually an old one. A caution, however: many pieces are being imported now from countries like Portugal, where hand labor is cheap. The pieces are set with rose diamonds, in silver, and they ape old pieces closely, even to the handwork lavished on mountings. These are reproductions, though, and should not be bought or sold as antique pieces—though they often are. Watch for them.

Synthetic stones first hit the market around 1880, and they were considered a great scientific achievement. Synthetic rubies were the first, and they are often seen in rings of that period. They look like real rubies, but have a slightly more electric pinkish-red color, and under the black light they glow (as natural rubies do), but a bit more brightly. If you have the two together, you can easily see the difference. Synthetic rubies are chemically the same, but are not as valuable as real rubies. But they do help to date a piece: they should not appear in a piece that was made prior to 1880.

There are many other synthetic (and frankly fake) stones, but it would take a gemological treatise to cover them all, and sophisticated equipment for you to recognize them. If you are buying a piece whose major value lies in its stones, have a reliable gemologist appraise it, or take it to the Gemological Institute on 47th Street in New York City where, for a reasonable sum, the stones will be studied and a report (not an appraisal) given to you on their nature and origin.

Cultured pearls were first produced by a Japanese noodle-peddler, Mikimoto, who patented a process in 1896 for inducing blister pearl formations by cementing a bit of mother-of-pearl inside an oyster's shell. (The Mikimoto

Company, still in the cultured pearl business, has just opened up a store on Fifth Avenue in New York City.) By the 1920s, cultured pearls were so popular and widely distributed that ingenious methods had to be devised to tell them from natural (or "oriental") pearls, since on the surface they appear exactly the same. Oriental pearls, however, have much greater value. Again, if you are in doubt and need to know if pearls are cultured or oriental, a gemologist or the Gemological Institute can perform tests, take X rays, and give you an answer. However, it is safe to say that pearls that are in their original settings on nineteenth-century pieces should be "oriental"; they predate Mr. Mikimoto.

Fake pearls, made of glass with fish scales or other pearlescent substances inside them, are really quite easy to tell from real pearls. One home-style method is to run your tooth over a pearl; real pearls tend to be grainy; glass pearls are smooth. With your loupe you can easily see the graininess—you don't have to run the risk of popping germy pearls in your mouth. If you look at pearls at all, you will soon see that glass pearls do not look or feel like real ones—the weight and luster are quite different, truly—and you will not worry about being fooled.

Distinguishing cultured pearls from oriental pearls is quite another thing: a matter for experts to determine, and not for you and me. Some dealers have told me that by holding cultured pearls up to a strong light, they can see the solid center in a cultured pearl and thus know the difference. But some cultured pearls, notably Biwas, are induced in the oyster by transplanting a bit of *flesh,* rather than shell, into it. This flesh is ultimately absorbed, and the Biwa, though cultured, is "all pearl." The "candling" test is really like a paternity test; if you see a solid center, you know your pearl is not oriental, but if you see nothing, you really still know nothing!

Seed pearls are the tiny real pearls that the Victorians liked to string (on horsehair) around stones or cameos, or onto mother-of-pearl backings to form parures (often earrings, pins, bracelets, and necklaces), or even in multiple strands to grace their throats. They are typically nineteenth century and are rarely used nowadays. These freshwater pearls have a special whiteness, different from that of other kinds of pearls. But most of all, they have to be strung, tediously, by hand, because the holes are so infinitesimal, and if they are ever broken, they are the very devil to repair. In an age when handwork is terribly expensive, it is even hard to find a craftsman willing to do it. To jewelry repairmen, seed pearls are not worth stringing, and so—although they are still around—seeing them used in any profusion on a piece nearly always stamps it as old. The delicate seed pearl parures usually date to the first half of the nineteenth century; seed pearls as a border hung on in popularity for some time after that.

There are certain stones so characteristic of Victorian jewelry that they deserve special attention. Among these are opals, turquoises, rock crystal, cairngorms, moonstones, garnets, peridots, amethysts, topaz, cat's-eye, and the various chalcedonies or agates (usually used to denote striped or banded stones): carnelian (red striped or orangey red), rose quartz (milky pink), onyx (black or dark brown, sometimes striped or in the form of an "eye"), jasper (reddish brown), bloodstone (green with red flecks), chrysoprase (green, preferably apple green), and moss agate (whitish with greenish or dark patterns like moss).

Opals have been known since Roman times; there is a story about a Roman senator, Nonnius, who chose exile rather than part with a large opal that Marc Antony coveted. In the early nineteenth century, opals were considered bad luck stones, perhaps because of Sir Walter Scott's popular novel *Anne of Geierstein,* in which the heroine, who loves opals, comes to a terrible flaming death. More than likely, the "bad luck" legend was enhanced by the fact that opals demand more care than most stones, and you are likely to have bad luck and ruin them. They are easily broken and—because the layer of opal in its matrix is usually thin, and consequently the polished stones are usually thin—very easily chipped. Even extremes in temperature can crack them, and so you should never expose your opal jewelry to very cold weather, leave it (or wear it) in direct hot sunlight, or wear opal rings in hot dishwater or while handling freezing food. Cold also shrinks opals, so check them in their settings if you suspect they have gotten too chilly! Opals are absorbent; if you wear them in the presence of dye or dirt (even dirty dishwater), they are likely to absorb impurities and be spoiled. And if that were not enough they *contain* water, which is an important factor in their play of colors. If opals "dry out" they "die"—and lose their iridescent fire. Oh, yes—they're also soft and scratch easily. (No wonder that they were considered hard luck stones! The miracle is that any old opal jewelry with its original stones intact has survived at all.)

Queen Victoria, however—that practical, sensible lady—gave no houseroom to the bad luck stories (she probably never washed any dirty dishes). She loved opals and promoted their popularity. Certainly she was influenced by the fact that the richest opal mines in the world were discovered in the British Empire—in Australia, in 1849. Victoria's enthusiasm for opals was substantiated by the Art Nouveau movement, which loved iridescence, and—on this side of the Atlantic—by Tiffany, whose fascination with iridescence in glass extended to enameling and gemstones as well. So the world forgot that opals were supposed to be "bad luck," and raised them to a popularity that they still enjoy today.

If you buy old opal jewelry, look carefully at the stones through your loupe to see what condition they are in, and if they are original to the piece. Despite what anyone may tell you, opals are very difficult to repolish because they are so fragile; hence, if you buy a ring with a very worn stone, don't expect miracles, and don't pay the price you would pay for a stone in good condition. On the other hand, opals are fairly plentiful, are still cut in the same way (cabochon) as they were in the nineteenth century, and are relatively easy to replace; so if you like a piece and everything else is right, you might consider replacing a worn or chipped opal. (If a stone has to be matched for size or color, however, that adds to the problem, and you should consider this as well.)

Because they are often so thin, opals are sometimes glued to a cheaper stone backing and set into rings or pins, usually with a closed mounting (so the trick is hard to discern). These are called "doublets," and although not precisely a cheat, a doublet (or even triplet) should be identified to you, and should not be passed off as—or command the same price as—a stone that is opal through and through.

Opals come in a variety of colors, and their price depends on size, depth, fineness of color, and degree of fire. Black opals (really more like a dark peacock blue, or slate gray, with flashes of yellows, reds, and greens), which were discovered only in 1903, and therefore should never be found or set in earlier jewelry, are the most costly. I prefer some of the older varieties with milky white, or pinkish-white, greenish, or bluish body color, or *water opals,* which are sometimes confused with moonstones—watery-clear base color with a flash of yellow or red or green, all of them showing as you turn it. *Fire opals*— yellowy-red stones without the broken-up bits of fire of the Australian opals— come from Mexico, and *harlequin opals,* truly magnificent plays of brilliant points of color, are mined in Czechoslovakia.

If you own and love opals, you should give them a long, luxurious bath now and then in water, or a mixture of glycerine and water, to keep them from drying out and losing their fire. They are great, fragile beauties that demand some care but give a lot of joy and pleasure in return.

Turquoise is a stone that has fascinated many cultures, including, of course, our own Southwestern Indians. The early and mid-Victorians were very fond of it, in round little cabochons, pavé set, or massed in lines and circles on rings or pins or bracelets. I have seen early Victorian snake necklaces and bracelets with turquoise "scales," and many Etruscan-style pins and earrings with dots or circles of bright turquoise in the center.

Like opal, turquoise is a porous stone, and it tends to change color as it gets older and is exposed to dirt or grease. Many old pieces pavé set with turquoise show several different colors of blue and green; they were probably beautifully matched when the piece was new. It is also easy to replace turquoise stones (either with the real thing or with several common substitutes), and so often *all* the turquoises in a piece are not original; you should check for this before buying. (Actually, my skepticism would be more easily aroused by a piece that looked too evenly matched than by one which showed the slight color variations of age.)

The most desirable turquoise color is a pure sky blue; the finest material of this color comes from Persia, and is relatively high-priced and rare. Greenish turquoise is more common. American turquoise is lighter colored and more porous than Eastern turquoise, and more often shows matrix; American Indians liked and valued larger pieces, and also that mosaic look. Fake turquoise is made of glass (and has been since antiquity), or dyed agate, or of artifically pressed materials (sometimes turquoise dust). True turquoise of poor color is sometimes dyed to look like finer material, but a bit of ammonia applied to the surface will remove the dye and expose the true color (a daring practice if the piece is not yours!). Hydrochloric acid dropped on bonded fake turquoise will turn greenish yellow, but it will also spoil the finish, and so it should be used only if you can find an inconspicuous place on the piece. With most Victorian pieces, the individual turquoise stones are so small that these methods are last-ditch actions; if you try them, be prepared to replace the fake stones with real turquoise should you discover any fakes, or you will have ruined your piece.

I have heard that the true color of turquoise can be restored by burying it in the earth, but to be truthful I have never tried this method. I rather like—and am comforted by—the play of turquoise colors in an antique piece, and what it tells me about the years of wear the stones enjoyed.

Turquoise is soft and easily scratched. It is almost never faceted, and it feels warm and rather "fat" to the touch.

Moonstones are a gem variety of feldspar—a grayish watery stone, always cabochon cut, that shows a shimmery white or blue sheen as you turn it in the light. The bluer the sheen, the finer the moonstone.

In the late nineteenth century, colored stones were passé, and moonstones, diamonds, and pearls were favored. Many of the Victorian moonstone pieces that you will see can be dated from that period—especially if they are light and delicate in appearance.

Moonstones interested Art Nouveau designers, too. In fact, all stones with "schiller" or "chatoyancy" (that play of sheen) did—and cat's-eye (a yellow-brown chrysoberyl), tiger's-eye (a darker brown banded quartz stone), and even humble feldspar (chalky gray-white with chatoyant "threads") shared in that turn-of-the-century popularity.

Garnets, peridots, amethysts, topaz, and colored stones of all kinds were pleasing to the mid-Victorians. Victorian rings set with many little stones of different or contrasting colors are getting hard to find now, but have a special period charm and are well worth looking for. Red pyrope or "Bohemian" garnets were popular with Middle Europeans, and many fine pavé-set garnet rings, earrings, pins, and bracelets (usually mounted in silver) were worn during the nineteenth century. Garnet jewelry very like that is still made in Europe today, and can be bought in ethnic shops in large American cities, but now it is usually mounted in gold. Almandine garnets—purply red—were also beloved by the Victorians; almandines are usually more simply cut, not highly faceted, like the Bohemian garnets, and are considered finer. Deep red garnets, cabochon-cut like great drops of aspic, were called carbuncles; they grace many beautiful Victorian pieces. More rare are demantoid (green) garnets and spessartite (reddish-brown). The demantoids are really quite valuable and hard to find.

Nowadays, garnets are rarely cut *en cabochon,* and so the old cabochons are hard to replace. You can tell garnets from rubies in a number of ways, but using a black light is easiest—rubies will glow red; garnets will not. Today pyrope garnets are among the most inexpensive of stones, but in my view their price has nothing to do with their beauty, which is great, and everything to do with their availability, which is also great.

Peridot is a yellowish green stone that was beloved in the late nineteenth century, but is not much in fashion today. The stone is a beauty, however, if the color is good. Peridots were often used on lavalieres in combination with pearls and diamonds: an elegant play of color and sheen. Peridots are found in old rings, too, but look at them carefully because peridot is a soft stone that wears easily. It is a rather unusual stone, not seen so often as some of the others.

Amethyst, on the other hand, is one of the commonest semiprecious stones. It is a quartz stone, clear purple in color. The finer the amethyst, the deeper and purer the purple. Amethyst is sometimes heat-treated to improve its color; *untreated* natural stones show a play of bluish and reddish tones, and this is very desirable.

Amethysts have been popular since earliest times and are still favorites today. The Victorians especially enjoyed amethysts surrounded by seed pearls or with small golden flowers engraved on them. The Art Nouveau movement appreciated the variety of forms and colors in amethysts and used them cut *en cabochon,* flawed, or even in their natural crystal forms, especially in combination with silver.

Yellow topaz was a great favorite in the eighteenth century, but lost ground in the nineteenth. Perhaps it was partly because of the confusion about topaz; at one time every yellowish or brownish yellow stone was called "topaz."

To further confuse the picture, *citrine* (which is a yellow quartz stone, similar in composition to amethyst and rock crystal) is often mislabeled "topaz." When you are shown a piece, therefore, and told it is topaz, make sure to ask if it is true natural gem topaz. Gem topaz is far more valuable than its quartz lookalikes. The most favored color for topaz today is a sherry brown, but the nineteenth century liked *pink topaz,* too, and used it often. (Pink topaz occurs naturally, but is rare; often clear topaz is heat-treated to produce the pink color.) *Cairngorm,* a clear brown quartz stone, which is much beloved and used in Scottish jewelry, is also sometimes confused with topaz. It is not the same.

Rock crystal—water-clear, colorless quartz—is an interesting stone, rarely used today but dear to our ancestors. I have already described (in chapter three) how to distinguish it from glass, which it resembles. It also resembles clear paste (a kind of glass) and, to some small degree, diamonds. Rock crystal is colder and harder than paste (and glass), and it does not display the fire of diamonds (or even zircons). When old pastes are set and foiled *en pavé,* each one shows a black dot at its center; rock crystal was not set in the same way, and does not show this dot. Most of the rock crystal you will see will probably be from the twenties—beads, perhaps earrings, or a pin or ring. If you are very lucky, however, perhaps you will chance on an eighteenth-century memorial ring, black or white enameled, with the name of the dear departed set in gold around the shank, and with a rock crystal stone. Rock crystal was used often on old memorial rings and brooches or even to front memorial lockets that held hair or other beloved relics. It was also carved into wonderful seals (nearly a dead art nowadays) and other small pieces. If you find one of these, and it is real rock crystal—not glass—count yourself lucky!

The use of *agates* in old jewelry could take up a whole chapter—a whole book, even—and still the surface would barely be scratched. They are so varied, occur in so many kinds of jewelry, and were so beloved that it is hard to know where to begin to talk about them.

Carved agates, for seals, cameos, charms, and the like, have been popular since Greek and Roman times. In the nineteenth century, with the rediscovery of so much classical art, there was a new vogue for carved agate. Intaglio seals were popular—with the patterns cut into the stone—and "stone cameos" carved from black and white (onyx) or red and white (carnelian) agates so that the white part of the stone stood out "in relief" from the darker part. (Shell cameos, carved in Italy, were popular in the nineteenth century, too, and for similar reasons.)

Today old *stone cameos* are, in general, more highly valued than shell cameos, and much harder to find. When you do find them, they are generally set in gold, as lockets, brooches, or rings, and they usually date from the first half of the nineteenth century. The aspect of the woman on the cameo is a clue to dating: the more simple, "classical" heads—and men's heads, if you can find them—are generally earlier. Fussier Victorian ladies with heavy necks and rather matronly airs usually belong to mid-century. Later, sensuous Art Nouveau sirens and Gibson Girl delicacy show up on cameos, but expect these to be shell, not stone.

If you are buying a stone cameo, check first of all to make sure that no part of the stone is chipped or cracked. You can run your fingernail around the edge of the piece for a preliminary check, but by far the best thing is to study the piece carefully under your loupe. This kind of detailed examination will also reveal the quality of the carving to you. A fine piece should be carefully and exquisitely carved, with all the detail perfect. The artist should make good use of his material, employing the contrast of dark and light (or, if the piece happens to be malachite, coral, or some other marked material, the natural markings) as an integral part of the design. In agate stone cameos, the artist can often use the semitranslucent nature of the white stone to get wonderful delicate effects—diaphanous folds of garments, lacy flowers or trees, delicate "see-through" lace collars, and the like. In general, a fine cameo carving stands high off its background. Sometimes three colors are achieved: the dark background, the "picture" carved in the light color, and a bit of "rind" or outer color on the highest part of the relief, perhaps in a lady's hair or the curled outer edges of flower petals. On very special pieces, the carving may be "undercut" so that the subject stands out from the background almost as though it were in the round.

Ancient cameos from Greek and Roman days are still to be found, and are very desirable. Sometimes these were reset by the Victorians into newer mountings, but the Victorians also imitated the ancients. You would probably need the advice of an expert to know if a "classic" cameo in a nineteenth-century frame really dated to antiquity.

In addition to the cameo itself, the price of a piece will be determined by the mounting. Is it gold, or gold filled? Has it been repaired? Is it of fine workmanship and suitable to the piece? Is it old? Is this the original cameo, or have a cameo and a mounting been "mismatched" to make one piece of jewelry?

The opposite of cameo carving is *intaglio carving*—the motif does not stand up from the stone, but is incised into it. The art of intaglio carving, too, has been practiced since ancient times; the earliest seals we know of—made of clay—go back to 6500 B.C., and since about 3000 B C stone seals have been engraved with their owner's mark. The Egyptians wore signet rings, as did the Greeks and Romans. By the seventeenth century the fob seal, one that was made to be hung on a chain or attached to a man's chatelaine, was a popular and useful piece of masculine jewelry. Both the fob seal and the signet ring have continued to be popular into modern times, although nowadays few craftsmen remain who can cut a seal by hand.

Many, though far from all, old seals were cut into agate. Carnelian was especially popular; so were bloodstone, jasper, rock crystal, and amethyst. I have an old *glass* seal in a brass mounting that says (in reverse, of course, so that its impression in wax would read correctly): "Pray without ceasing." It is worth perhaps ten or fifteen dollars, but it is wonderful; I wouldn't part with it! I have another that shows, in incredibly precise, tiny details, a clock face, and bears the words (in carnelian, this time, set in 15K gold): "Le temps passe; la amtie [sic] reste." It dates from the first half of the nineteenth century and reflects the British duality in their feelings about the French: French was "classy," the language of love and all that—but English was better, and so casually but inevitably, a word of the French was characteristically misspelled.

Men's watch charms of all kinds and lockets and doodads show up in antique shops constantly. Many of them are agate and date to the last half of the nineteenth century. I have seen agate compasses, lockets with agate sides, agate-handled glove hooks, agate-beaded fobs, all fascinating and all worth collecting.

Agates were used for a host of other things, too. Scottish jewelry made of gold or, more usually, of silver, with beautifully cut and polished agates set into it, was beloved of Queen Victoria and therefore popular during the middle of the nineteenth century. Brooches in the shape of love knots or anchors (the symbol of "hope"), circles or dirks (Scottish daggers) or butterflies; lockets set with agate; sectioned bracelets of long pieces of agate capped with gold or silver, and sometimes set off with a heart-and-key closure; agate beads and locket chains; and—rarely—agate earrings; all were popular and beloved.

10. Scotch agate

Most often the metal was handsomely hand-chased around the agates, and often the central or most important stone (particularly on the thistle-headed dirks) was an amethyst or a cairngorm. The agates in these pieces are multi-colored—reds and mustardy golds and dark greens and grays and banded blacks—but often a piece will have matched agates of a single color, soft feathery gray or banded brown. Often, too, the same styles were wrought in malachite (a beautiful green-banded stone that depends on copper for its characteristic color); these pieces usually date a bit earlier.

If you find a beautiful old Scottish agate piece in silver, with all the agates original (run your fingernail around them for chipping and un-evenness; check with your loupe for signs of glue or reset stones) and in good condition, you are in luck. If the piece is mounted in gold, and the price is not absolutely astronomical, you have a "find." Good agate earrings are really rare; I wish I had bought the only fine, perfect, reasonably priced pair I was ever offered. Be careful, though, not to confuse the old pieces with similar newer pieces being made in England and Scotland and sold now. These are not reproductions, but a continuation of an old tradition, as new Irish "clad-dagh" (clasped hands beneath a heart) rings are a continuation of an ancient marriage ring motif. The new pieces have rounded baroque pebbles and are much more crudely made than the old ones. The mountings are generally cast, and the work on them is nothing like the careful old hand engraving on the Victorian ones. If you are in doubt, *ask;* few dealers would have the nerve—or the inexperience—to pass off a new Scotch pebble piece for an Old Victorian Scotch agate treasure.

Scotch agates do *not* appeal to everyone, but if they are your "thing," they are well worth collecting. The fine perfect ones are getting rarer and harder to come by every day, and their price is climbing. Pieces that sold for five or ten dollars a decade ago are bringing ten times that much (or more) today, and there is no reason to think that prices will come down. These Scottish pieces are rare; they're genuinely old; they're specific to the period; they're beauti-ful—and they look wonderful with today's styles, colors, and fabrics.

Chapter Eight

How to Wear and Take Care of Old Jewelry: Some Practical Dos and Don'ts

Buying a fine, authentic piece of old jewelry is only a beginning. Wearing it, storing it, handling it, and maintaining it properly so that its value will not be lost but will be enhanced by your owning it—these things become your responsibility and pleasure from the moment you pay over your money and take possession. To begin with, when the seller hands you your new treasure, make sure it is protected in a piece of tissue, a bag of plastic or paper, or—best of all—a box.

Jewelry that is properly maintained will gain in value. Anything that takes its value from its age can only gain by getting older. You have seen, I'm sure, horrible examples of careless maintenance—broken and chipped pieces, discolored materials, bent and broken mountings, and so on. It is my hope that no one who reads this book will commit such atrocities on beautiful old survivors of times past. However, it takes a little knowledge for you to do your best for the jewelry that does its best for you.

Each piece of jewelry you own must be *stored separately,* preferably in its own box. If that is impossible for space or other reasons, store it in its own compartment of your jewelry box or in plastic or cloth bags. Plastic baglets that seal with a rub of your fingernail can be bought cheaply in jewelry supply houses or hobby shops, and these are very good for storing most jewelry. Since they are transparent, they help you to find your pieces easily, and if you store in a vault or home safe, they have the added advantage of taking up very little space. Very soft or fragile pieces, like delicately wired coral earrings, should have more protection than a small plastic bag can give. Some materials, like pearls and opals and ivory, need to "breathe" occasionally, and so should not be stored in plastic indefinitely. For such materials, cloth bags or hard-sided boxes are best. Don't be tempted to put more than one piece in a bag; this can lead to disaster. Stones can chip and break jostling against one another. Soft materials like ivory, turquoise, or glass are easily scratched by harder ones. Low karat gold, which is tough, will scratch and mar softer high karat gold. Rings, especially, with all their stones and delicate goldwork, will be in bad trouble if they are jumbled together. Enameled pieces cannot survive being jostled; once enamel cracks or chips, its value is drastically reduced, and it can never really be successfully restored to its original condition.

I have a few friends who have a habit of simply dropping their jewelry into a jewelry box. Just thinking about the damage being done to wonderful old (or new) pieces by this barbaric behavior gives me cold chills. And when, on a dealer's counter, I see the poor crippled old pieces—cracked agates, mosaics with bits missing, scratched and dented lockets, broken pin backs, and the like—and the dealer offers me that old saw about "If you were as old as this, you'd be dented/scratched/worn/imperfect, too," I think: "Maybe. But if I'd been as badly treated as that piece has been, I wouldn't be around at all!"

The best way to store a ring is in a ring box, which can be bought at jewelry supply houses. If you don't have a jewelry supply source in your area, perhaps your jeweler, or the dealer you buy from, will get a box for you. If your dealer friends are not that accommodating, or if you're on a budget or would rather spend your money on jewelry itself than on boxes, you can easily improvise a fine ring box from a cigar box (or any box with a good lid) lined with foam rubber. Carefully cut slits (in even rows) just long enough to hold your rings, and keep the rings this way, one to a slit. A really fancy job might include pasting velvet (appropriately slitted) to the foam rubber, but that's just window dressing. The important thing is that each ring should be held firmly, out of contact with every other ring.

Another way to store rings is in a partitioned box (also easy to make if your local variety store or hobby store can't supply one)—one ring to a compartment. Sometimes department stores will offer jewelry cases of beautiful silky fabrics or of leather, with spaces for rings, pins, necklaces, and other pieces; but I find these inadequate. The jewelry slips around in the case, is hard to find, and is hard to keep separate. I prefer the homelier, surer methods.

Pins and brooches can be kept in boxes, in compartments, or in plastic bags, too—or they can be carefully pinned to velvet-covered cardboard or wooden pads that will fit, one on top of the other, into a sturdy box. These, too, can be easily and effectively homemade.

Chains, of course, can be kept in the same ways as other pieces, or—if you have a convenient spot near your dressing area—they can be hung on nails padded with a bit of felt or felt-faced Contac paper. As you accumulate more pieces, you may find it cumbersome to store all of them in bureau drawers. At that point it is time to investigate renting a safety deposit box in your local bank and keeping at least part of your collection there.

In big cities and busy suburbs there is always the danger of theft. Often robbers, seeing antique jewelry instead of the more readily negotiable diamonds, solid gold, and the like, will break it up or mutilate it. That is almost more heartbreaking to a passionate collector than having the pieces stolen altogether. A friend of mine who has a great deal of jewelry advises hiding most of your pieces and leaving a few gold articles of lesser value around to be stolen. Her thought is that if burglars find no jewelry, they will be suspicious and search (and vandalize) your house, but that they will accept a few pieces if you leave them around like votive offerings. I detest this idea. A better technique is to keep most of your jewelry securely in your bank vault, and find a good and unusual hiding place in the house for the rest of it. Thieves know about the clothes hamper, the freezer, and the washing machine, so don't try those. I have another friend who takes the "hiding route," but is absentminded; at any given time, she is hunting down some treasure that, like a dog with a bone, she hid and can't dig up again. In general, antique jewelry is not as easy to "fence" or to break up and sell for the value of the stones and the gold as valuable modern stone jewelry, so it is not as attractive to robbers. But it still does get stolen and, realistically, must be protected.

How about insurance? Most insurance companies include a nominal amount of coverage for the theft of personal possessions if they insure your house or apartment. This sum is usually very small—$250, perhaps. It would hardly cover the loss of a collection of any size at all. Furthermore, most insurance companies are very insensitive to the value of antique jewelry; they will often insist that they can "replace" a piece for you with another of equal value in stones and gold. They refuse to understand that the value of an old piece does not rest totally or even primarily on the size of its stones and the karat of its gold, but on its age, beauty, condition, and so on. As for appraisals, check with your insurance agent to make sure, but most insurance companies will pay only a percentage of the appraised value; they assume your appraisal has been "kited up" (which indeed it may have been), and will not honor the total amount. If, however, the appraisal is more than a year or so old, no matter how much it may originally have been "kited," your piece may easily be worth much more, and you will be badly shortchanged by your insurance company if you should have to collect on it.

There is a way of taking a "floater" policy with your company that will insure each piece of your jewelry separately. This is very expensive insurance, and also a big bother if your collection is large, as the company will probably want a picture, description, and appraisal of every piece they insure. It seems to me that a safety deposit box and careful, secure handling are a better kind of "insurance" for antique jewelry than any other.

Never, never store your jewelry in a very damp or very dry place, in direct sunlight, near a heat source, or in a very cold place. Many materials are sensitive to temperature and humidity and can be ruined in this way. In my bank, some of the safety deposit boxes must back up on a heat source; I found my valuables *warm* when I took them out of the vault, and asked to have my box location changed.

If you do keep your jewelry in the vault, make sure to visit it occasionally, wind your watches, take your pearl and opal and ivory pieces out to check their condition and let them "breathe"; take your opals home to soak them from time to time, and examine all your pieces for missing stones, changes in the color of the materials, drying out, shrinking, cracking, warping, and so on. Sometimes jewelry acts like machines (and people)—it thrives with use, but quickly deteriorates if it is neglected. Many pearl lovers swear that the luster of their pearls improves with wear. Opals certainly "warm up" in color when they are on your finger or against your throat, and certain jades intensify in color, or even change color, when they are worn. The oil in watches tends to gum up and clog movements that are not running; telling time is *good* for watches. Some experts say that amber tends to go cloudy and dark after long exposure to air. If this is so, it would certainly be better to store amber that is not regularly worn in a dark place, with controlled temperature and humidity.

Old portraits are often crotchety and need special attention. Portraits on ivory are subject to mold and fungus damage, cracking, splitting, fading, curling, and other horrors. If you own an ivory portrait, *never* use anything but a rouge cloth on the outside. It's hard to believe—but I have seen beautiful portraits with hair lockets that were actually dipped in jewelry cleaner or smeared with runny metal polish. Needless to say, the liquid seeped into the hair and portrait compartments and they were irretrievably ruined. (Never buy such a flawed piece unless you absolutely can't resist it, and never believe a dealer who tells you it can be repaired; it can't.)

Store portraits in cool, dark places where the humidity is constant—not too damp, not too dry. Portraits that are painted on other surfaces—paper (sometimes even old calling cards or playing cards), wood, or the like—demand the same care as ivory. Porcelain or enameled portraits are waterproof, and therefore not as sensitive to humidity, heat, and cleaning problems, but they do chip easily and cannot be repaired. All enamel, porcelain, and Wedgwood pieces should be kept in separate boxes (if that is impossible, in separate plastic or cloth bags) and swathed in cotton or tissue paper.

Silver, of course, has a tarnish problem. It is actually the sulfur in the air that does the "dirty work" on silver—and back in the days before industrialization, this was not much of a problem at all. In these polluted times, it is best to keep your silver jewelry in airtight plastic bags. I have never used the specially impregnated tarnish-retardant cloth that is made for tableware, but theoretically it seems as though that would keep jewelry tarnish free, too. However, I would be careful of using it with other more delicate materials that might be combined with the silver—turquoise or pearls or portraits or tortoise—for fear of what the unknown "miracle" chemicals might do to these sensitive substances. Silver against silver usually does not scratch (since all sterling silver is the same alloy), but silver can be dented or marred in other ways; so, as a rule, I keep each silver piece, too, in its own separate cubby.

Just two more perhaps redundant tips about storing jewelry. First, when I travel, I always carry *on my person* whatever (minimal) jewelry I am taking along. I don't trust it to hotel rooms, airlines, or locked cars—and it's not only human beings that I fear. The belly of an airliner, where the luggage is stored, is below freezing temperature; locked cars can become hotboxes in the summertime or iceboxes in the winter. I carry my jewelry in my pocketbook, carefully stored, plastic bag by plastic bag and then consolidated into one larger purse or "baggie"; that way I know where it is and what it is experiencing. (If I take along very little jewelry, I wear it—that is the best storage of all!) Second, when I take a piece out of its box or plastic bag, I always do so over a soft surface (such as a bed or a tablecloth) so that if my hands slip I will not send an old friend crashing to the hard floor; I also always examine the piece, check the stones, and carefully shake out the bag or box over the same surface to make sure that no broken bit of jewelry or dislodged gemstone is still hiding inside. If you get into the habit of putting each piece away as soon as you take it off, and of scrupulously checking it and its cubby when you get ready to wear it, you will rarely, if ever, lose irreplaceable bits and pieces of your treasures.

Wearing old jewelry is an art in itself. As I have said, very old brooches may have been made to be sewn to dresses and hats, and if they have not already been "modernized," you may need some ingenuity to make them wearable today. They can successfully be sewn to a stiffened velvet backing, which then can be fitted with a modern pin. This sewing must be done very securely, however, or you will lose the brooch. Perhaps a better way, if the old piece will adapt itself to it, is to string it on a velvet ribbon or a gold chain and wear it as a pendant. In whatever you do, remember how delicate these old survivors are. Also, don't change or remove any part of them if you can possibly help it; you will spoil their originality and value.

Victorian brooches, with their long heavy pin and C-clasp, were made to be worn on heavy fabrics. When you attach them to a modern fabric or to a knitted sweater or dress, carefully *weave* the pin in and out a few times before engaging the clasp. Make sure the pin moves past the narrowest part of the C to rest secure in the curve. Then, if the tip of the pin protrudes past the edge of the brooch (the older the brooch, the further it generally protrudes), pass this tip *back into* the fabric; that is your "safety clasp." If the pinback is insecurely fastened, or if the spring has gotten weak with age, ask your jeweler for a *spring clutch,* and use it to hold the pin in place. Slip the pin through a bit of fabric, push on and secure the clutch, then add more fabric, and close the pin. If the pin opens, the clutch will hold your piece to your clothing. A clutch must be just the right size for the pin. If it is too small, it will not hold; if it is too large, it may bend your piece or break it. It is best, therefore, to take the brooch with you to the jewelers and try the clutch on for size.

Most Victorian brooches were made to be worn at the throat, and the balance of the piece is sometimes wrong if you wear it, as we do our modern ones, farther down and on one side. The pin was inserted from right to left (very rarely from top to bottom because that "safety" point would stab you if you wore it that way), and the oval was worn from side to side, not from top to bottom. These brooches look very handsome today on turtleneck sweaters or high-necked dresses, but are often wrong for low necklines, and will "pull" forward. They are too heavy to wear unless they are securely held by the fabric and "lean" against you. One trick is to slip a piece of ribbon inside your dress and pin the brooch—through the thin fabric—to the ribbon. Sometimes this will save the day.

Stickpins, which were originally intended to set off men's neckwear or women's scarves, should always be worn with a clutch slipped up securely behind them, to hold the pin in place. The pins themselves are often quite thick and will leave holes in today's lighter fabrics. My husband will not wear them except with knit ties. But they, too, are wonderful on sweaters or knit suits, and especially good in groups of two or three. Don't give in to any tasteless "jewelry redesigner" who offers to snip the long pins and make your stickpins into a tacky little "bouquet"; leave them as they are.

Turn-of-the-century brooches were just the opposite of the Victorian ones. Made to be worn on light silks and voiles, they often get lost on heavier fabrics and bright colors, and look inconsequential. They are best worn in twos and threes (except for the bar pins), and look pretty on shirt collars or turtlenecks that way. Small delicate brooches called "lace pins" look handsome worn *across* a gold chain, securing it at the side or in the center, like a love knot. Small brooches are usable as clasps, too; if you have a long strand of pearls, try using a small brooch this way, to "clasp" the strand into a double. Sometimes dealers are guilty of taking small, uninteresting pins that they can't sell and having them made into rings, which enjoy a livelier market. When you ask if the piece is old, they will answer yes with unblinking honesty. But if you ask if the top is old and the shank is new, they will usually tell the truth about it. Ask this question whenever you suspect that a ring has been "put together." Such a piece is neither good nor old; it is a mongrel, and unless you love it desperately, don't buy it.

Very small brooches can be pinned to a dark velvet ribbon and worn as a beautiful choker or bracelet. I know someone who puts snaps on the ends of velvet ribbons of various colors, and uses them with all her small pins, and even as hairbands and hatbands. It is an attractive idea.

It seems unnecessary to tell anybody how to wear *earrings,* and yet many old and beautiful earrings are spoiled and broken because they were improperly handled. First of all, most old earrings are made for pierced ears (the screwback was first used around 1890), and if your ears are not pierced, don't alter the earrings; alter *you!* Piercing, if it is done by an experienced careful person, is quick, safe, and does not hurt nearly as much as losing a pair of beloved earrings (or *one* of a pair, which is even worse).

To put on stud earrings correctly, place the fleshy part of your left forefinger behind your left ear, and carefully (looking in the mirror if you need to) push the pin of the earring through the hole with your right hand, guiding it with that left forefinger. (This is so easy for old-time ear-stud wearers that they will laugh to see it described, but if you have just had your ears pierced, getting a pair of earrings on can really be a problem.) Some women pull their ears down to make the holes easier to find; if you do this you will eventually stretch the skin, and it will look ugly.

In putting ear wires in from the front, more or less the same technique is used. It is important not to bend or force the wires open. If they seem too narrow, try putting them in absolutely horizontally, and "rolling them down" ninety degrees to hang properly in your ear. Once you get the feel of this, it will simplify greatly the problems of narrow, small ear wires that seem to pinch your lobe unbearably as you put them on. To take them off, do the same thing in reverse, rolling the wire from its up-and-down position in the ear to straight-across as you pull it through the earhole. Never force earrings; you will break or bend them, and it is not necessary. They were made to be worn and should be easily put on and taken off. To hook the little catches on the back, try using your fingernail and simply springing the wires forward and letting go. If they are properly made and have not been bent out of shape, they should spring back into locked position. If not, you will have to do them in the mirror, or get a cooperative husband or child to help you.

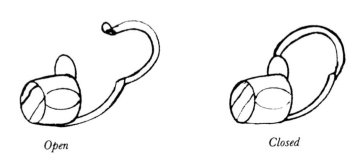

Open   Closed

11.   Front-closure earrings

Earrings that run from back to front are a little harder to manage. Again, feel for the hole in the back of your right ear with the thumb of your right hand, and then, with the earring back fully open, guide the earring (with your left hand) into the hole. The wire should enter at right angles to your ear. Your right middle finger can be in front of the earlobe, feeling for the wire and helping it to emerge in front of the lobe. Then, with the earring still at right angles, put your right thumb at the very bottom of the earring and press down gently on the top of the wire with your right forefinger. You should hear a little "snap": the lock of the earring engaging properly. Now pull a bit on the earring; it should stay locked. If it opens, roll the earring around so that it is again in a horizontal position (the lock facing down) and try that gentle press between your fingers again. You should not have to pry or bend the wire, or fuss excessively with the lock. If the earring is not bent, it should lock easily, as it was made to do. (Reverse this for the other ear.) If you have trouble locking these little back-to-front oldies, try doing it as I describe, but with the earring *out* of your ear. When you get the hang of it, you'll never break or bend your earrings, or lose them because they weren't closed securely. Sometimes these little earrings open with a fingernail touch that lifts the lock away from the wire, sometimes in other ways, but look at your earring carefully and try gently to discover how it was made to operate before you put it on. It should never be necessary to handle it roughly, bend the gold, or push the parts out of place.

A small earring with stones that are not affected by heat or water, and that locks securely, can certainly be worn day and night. I take mine off when I shower or swim only because I don't want to risk losing the stones, but there is no reason why you have to take them off when you sleep unless they are uncomfortable. Foiled stones, however, cannot take water and must be removed for showering; the same applies to ivory and hair. Earrings of very delicate material should be taken off at night—I certainly would not advise sleeping in fragile and elaborate wired coral earrings.

Victorian bracelets were usually made to fit on the wrist itself (not high on the arm), and often came in pairs, one to each wrist. Most fine gold bracelets and many silver ones were fitted with a safety chain, which protected the bracelet from loss if the clasp opened accidentally. If you own a bracelet without a safety chain, but with a small loop for one still on it, do invest the little it costs to have a safety chain added by your jeweler. This will in no way alter the piece or its value, but it may save you from a sad loss. (Brooches, too, sometimes have that little ring for a "safety": a bit of very fine chaining attached to a sort of safety pin. If you come across a piece like that in someone's junk box, you are in luck! They are rare and come in very handy, fulfilling their original function far better than a "clutch."

A word or two more about wearing bracelets: the function of a bracelet is to show off your hand. To this end, it should be of a becoming size and shape, suitable to you, your activities, and what you are wearing it with. If it is a bangle or a cuff bracelet, it should fit closely, following the contour of your wrist, and in the right position on your arm. Some people have a round wrist, some have a rather flat one; your bracelet and your wrist should be the same shape. If you prefer a chain link bracelet, find one that is the right size (or have a few links added or a few taken off—and safely kept) so that it fits snugly but not tightly, without too much jangling around.

If any links are added or taken off a gold bracelet, each link in the bracelet should end up securely gold-soldered, and the same holds for silver (and silver solder). I personally am bothered by charm bracelets or dangly additions to bracelets (maybe because I type so much), but many women love them—men do too—and find them becoming and pleasurable to wear. Breakable charms, though, of stone, glass, coral—anything that might be destroyed if "whonked"—should not be risked on bracelets. Many old watch chains are of just the right size to serve as charming bracelets, but beware of smashing those fine, dangly old watch fobs.

How to wear *rings*? Well, it doesn't seem very complicated, does it? But there are a few things you should know that will keep you and your rings from getting into trouble: When putting on an old ring, be especially careful not to force it over a knuckle that's too large for it. Old rings are fragile, and often the gold shank is worn thin. Breaks are sometimes hard or even impossible to repair, and a rebuilt old ring is no longer really original. The same caution applies to taking the ring off. If your hand has swollen, don't pull and twist the ring. Instead, raise the hand above your head for a few minutes and try again; the ring will probably come off without trouble. If it has no foiled stones or pearls, try a little cold water and soap, or some vaseline or oil, on your finger. The worst thing to do is to panic and try to pull a tight ring off— your finger will swell, and you'll end up cutting off the ring to save the finger.

Rings, like bracelets, have as their primary purpose to flatter your hand, and so you should choose them—in respect to color, shape, and size—so they will be as becoming as possible. There is no reason in the world why you should not wear as many rings as your hand will hold, provided you enjoy doing it—and they look well on you. Hoop rings of different stones are striking worn in twos and threes, separated perhaps by plain old gold wedding bands so that each stone ring is shown off. Rings with single stones in Tiffany settings are pretty worn in twos and threes, too. Or perhaps you like a hand full of snake rings, or mizpahs, or cameos. I have seen women who wear tiny baby rings on the first and second joints of their fingers, but these always seemed precarious to me. What happens if you shake hands with someone and your rings slip off?

I never have rings sized; I like to wear them on whatever finger they fit. If they are too big to fit a finger, I have a ring guard (a small strip of gold) placed inside the ring to make it fit tighter, and leave the size "as is." There is nothing really wrong with having a ring made larger or smaller so that it

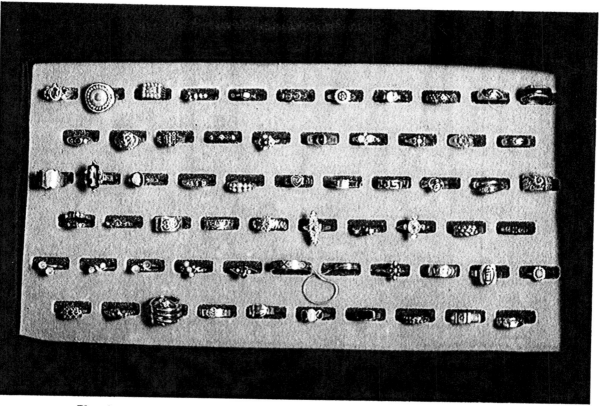

Plate 1. RINGS *Top row*. Several eighteenth-century rings and early nineteenth-century memorial rings with hair under crystal. *Second row:* A variety of Victorian rings with various settings; the last ring in this row was my grandmother's engagement ring; the one next to it is a synthetic ruby of around the same age (c. 1900) in a belcher setting. *Third row:* Two stone cameos, two REGARD rings (one with the colored stones set between pearls), three hair rings, and three nineteenth-century snakes. *Fourth row:* Various nineteenth-century rings, including an old keeper marked " '98" and a gemel ring with two hands that open to show a heart. *Fifth row:* Beautiful enameled handkerchief ring, a FEDE (faith) ring, and a MIZPAH ring. *Sixth row:* A beautiful five-turn snake with a diamond head and ruby eyes, buckle rings, a louseback (curved, flat on top and faceted underneath) garnet ring, and a few rings with gypsy settings.

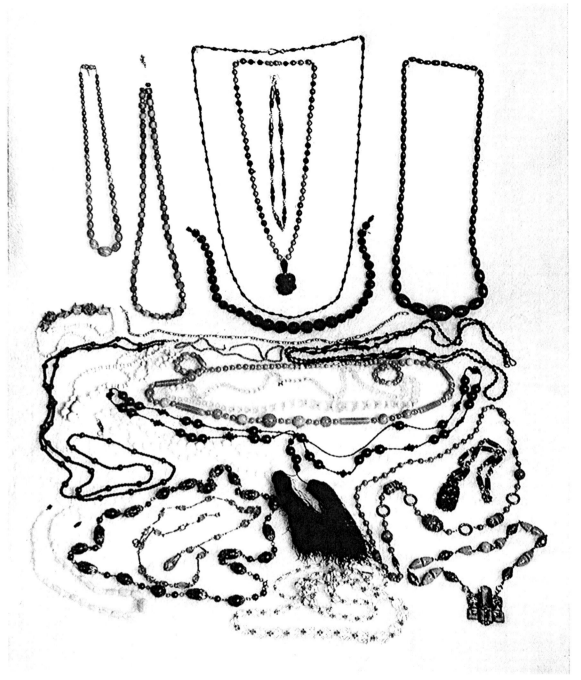

Plate 2.   BEADS The hanging beads are jets and ambers of various shades. The center amber necklace is of "butterscotch" and black amber with a pendant carved rose. Inside it is an English agate necklace capped with silver. Below it is a fine strand of carved jet.

Under the ambers, to the left, is a plastic imitation necklace (c. 1930) aping ivory and amber (compare this with the real thing for color). In the same "row" are gold beads (c. 1930), more jets (nineteenth century), and a handsome strand of long black Peking glass beads with knotted cord and tasseled fringes (c. 1920). Also satiny gypsum beads, babies' coral beads, ivory beads, and (in lower corners) glass-and-brass of the 1920s and 1930s, centered by a long handsome strand of glass "crystals." Note the *closures* and *lengths* of the various strands.

Plate 3. UNUSUAL MATERIALS *Top left.* Examples of tortoise and tortoise piqué; the handsome center chain is tortoise. *Top right.* Bog oak; below it, a glass mosaic framed in gold. Below that *(right)*, three pieces of bog oak (note the shamrocks carved in each one) and two jet earrings. Centered under the tortoise chain are a jet comb and pendant; to the left of it, two pieces of cut steel.

Under the bog oak pieces are a gutta-percha cloak clasp and two brooches of the same material. Also in the picture is a niello pencil, a niello watch chain, and a fine niello locket; jet mourning bracelets and carved jet beads; a stone cameo locket with a marvelous hair chain; a ruby glass brooch; agate and crystal circle pins and an agate locket and lock-and-key bracelet; two hands with roses, one of ivory and one of bone, plus a bone ivy carving—and a wealth of gunmetal pieces.

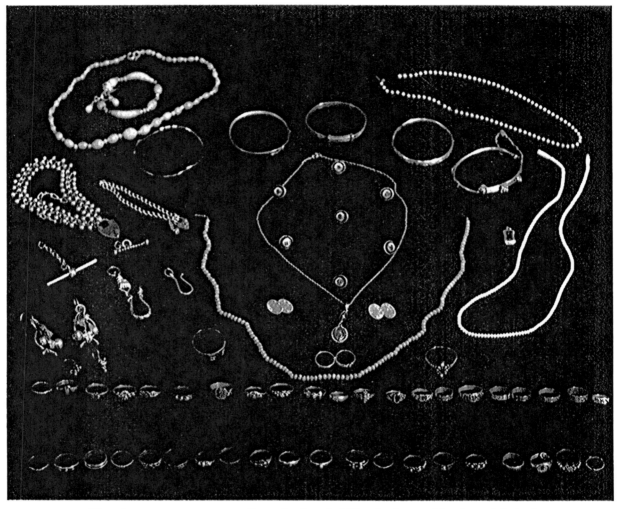

Plate 4. BABY JEWELRY A fine collection of children's pieces, with a few adult-sized pieces (rings, earrings, watch hook, and lock-and-key brocelet) to suggest the diminutive size of the collection. Pictured are tiny baby beads of coral, gold, and ivory plus a glass bracelet and necklace; mosaic buttons, small watch hook and bar, locket, opal pendant surrounded by seed pearls, gold cuff links, and a collection of fine baby rings.

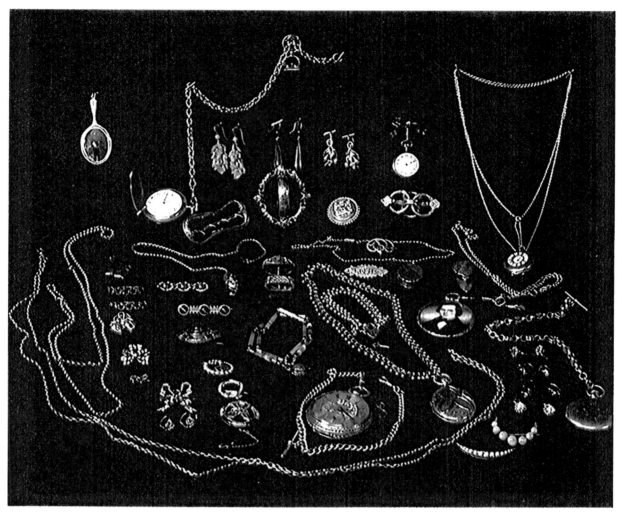

Plate 5.   HIGH VICTORIAN JEWELRY Some fine examples of typical nineteenth-century pieces: watch chains and watches (men's and ladies'); earrings; a "flirtation mirror"; a portrait on ivory (c. 1830) with hair compartment in the back; bar pins; bow pins; a coral half-moon brooch; agate lock-and-key bracelet; silver locket and bracelet; snake buckle; fine snake necklet with garnet heart (modern).

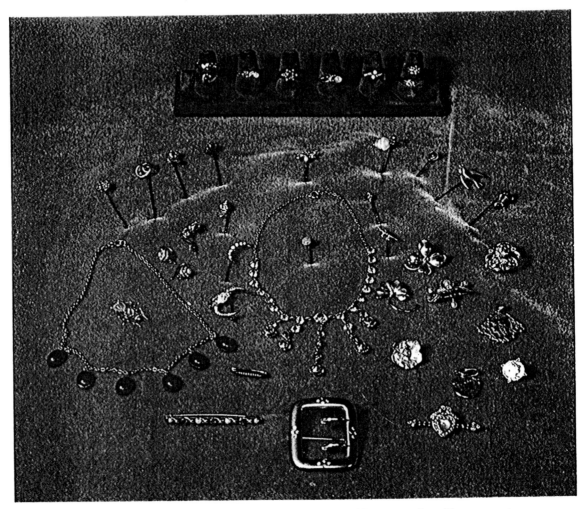

Plate 6. TYPICAL TURN OF THE CENTURY JEWELRY Rings, crystal necklace, garnet and gold necklace (c. 1910), pins, stickpins, and a collection of Art Nouveau brooches and slides.

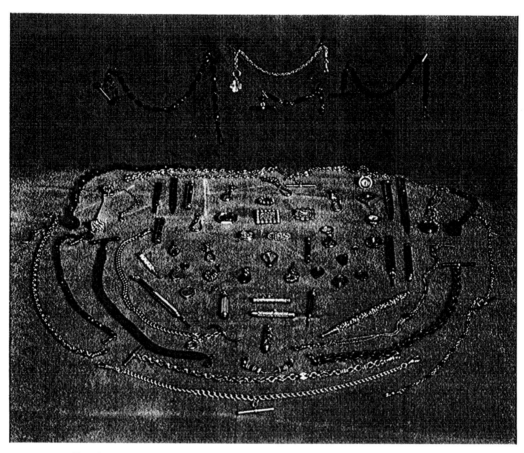

Plate 7. A COLLECTION OF COLLECTIONS A collection of watch chains and fobs in many materials: jet, silver, hair, glass, gold, gutta-percha, agate; a collection of locks and keys; a collection of mourning pins with pearls, crystals, coral, and other materials; a collection of watch hooks, buttonhooks, and compasses (all of which hung on watch chains); a collection of old pencils in various materials: silver, ivory piqué, papier-mâché, mother of pearl, gold, gold filled, vulcanite, and other materials.

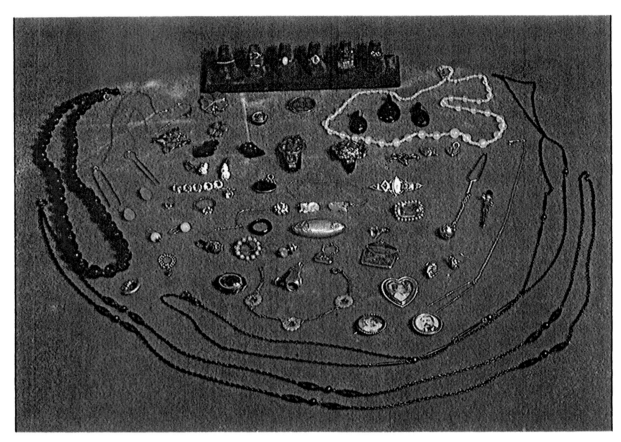

Plate 8. JEWELRY THAT COST $15 OR LESS (all bought during the last few years). Included are silver chatelaine hooks, glass beads, gunmetal chains, carved jet beads (restrung without original clasp), coral brooches, portrait brooches, an old brooch with paste aquamarine and pearls, glove hook, scotch agate dagger pin, faceted jet mourning ring, chain ring with heart locket inscribed "Gus to Amy, 1894"; sterling silver cigar cutter; "jade" glass bracelet (Art Deco); gold hairpins with original chaining and clasps; coral tie tack; enameled sterling silver sweater or shawl clasps (Art Deco); glass seal; crystal pin, crystal earrings, and crystal ring, all set in sterling. Other items: sterling heart pendants, opalescent glass beads, sterling name pins, gold watch pin, a sterling four-leaf clover pin marked "1890," and handmade jet mourning earrings (very early) with jet beads sewn to leather backing.

will fit you perfectly, providing that the work is done by a good and careful craftsman who knows something about old jewelry; that the ring has no enameling or carving around the shank, or marks that would be lost or spoiled by the sizing; and that the repair is made so well that nobody could ever tell that the ring had been worked on. If a ring is made much smaller, your jeweler should give you the gold he took out, or make a price adjustment for you; if it is made larger, you can be sure you will pay in full measure for the gold he puts in!

Fragile and delicate stones or rings that catch on clothing are best not worn on the first or pointer finger, as this is the finger that is most likely to be banged against things. Two bulky or wide rings, or two enameled rings, are best not worn on adjacent fingers; if they click against each other, they may

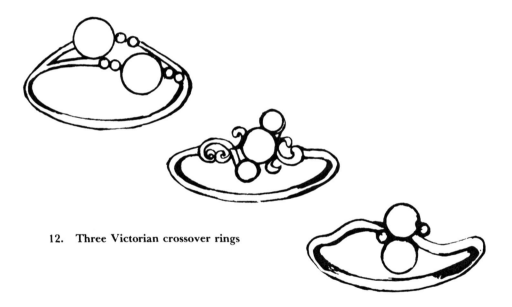

12.   **Three Victorian crossover rings**

harm each other. Rings that catch against each other should not be worn on one finger, or if they are, perhaps they can be separated by a plain gold band so that they will not interfere with each other.

The corresponding fingers of your two hands are not the same size, as perhaps you have already discovered; your writing hand is generally larger all around than its mate. In the summer your hand is larger than in the winter, when your fingers tend to shrink from the cooler atmosphere. Most people find that their fingers are larger (and hence their rings are tighter) when they get up in the morning and when they go to bed at night than they are during the middle of the day. You will also find out (if you haven't already) that as you get older your knuckles tend to get larger, and rings that once fit over them easily may not slip on at all anymore. Of course, we all know that when we lose or gain weight (or water, if the body tends to retain fluids), the fingers lose and gain, too.

What does all this have to do with old jewelry? Simply that when you choose a ring, or have it sized, these changes should be taken into account, and planned for. Nobody wants to size a ring in the winter and then have to size it again in the summer. In fact, the less you fuss with *any* old jewelry, the better. Think carefully about what finger you will wear your ring on, and what the changes will be, before you decide what size to make it. Fingers and rings have shapes, too, like wrists, and different rings of different widths fit differently. Never allow a jeweler to decide what size *your* ring should be from measuring you with *his* ring sizers. If all this sounds too complicated, you know now why I never size at all. Guards can be a nuisance, too—but they can be adjusted easily and, if necessary, taken off or put on just as easily.

Rings with opals, pearls, ivory, or turquoise stones need special care (see chapter seven), as do rings with foiled stones, hair rings, or rings with any kind of locket compartments. Moonstones, opals, pearls, turquoise, and pastes are easily scratched, and gold—especially high karat gold—is easily dented and bent. All these cautions cannot be repeated too often. Never, never wear your fine old rings when you are doing heavy or dirty work, gardening, painting, heavy housecleaning, and the like. Choose a very special place in your kitchen, one that your family knows about, where you can put your rings when dirty duties come up. Then you—and your family—will know where to look for them, and they will never wind up (as a friend's once did) in the bottom of a coffee cup! Make a practice, too, of having as many empty slots in your ring box as you have rings out of it. If you have more slots than rings, put pennies into them; if you have more rings than slots, get another ring box. That way, when you put your rings away at night, you will know immediately how many you took out that morning, and if any are missing, you can find them before you forget where you put them.

Old rings are very precious, and are getting more expensive and harder to find every day. Love and take care of yours, and they will give you a lifetime of pleasure and be a heritage for your children. Treat them roughly, and they will soon be nothing but bits and pieces of pathetic old gold.

Chains at this writing are probably the "hottest" item of antique jewelry. The prices of old ones have soared, more repros of old chains are around than of any other kind of piece (with the possible exception of rings), and women—

and men—are wearing chains with everything. If the chain you buy is in good condition and has no stones or enameling to worry about, there is little you need to do to keep it in good condition. Just inspect it from time to time to make sure that the links are all holding well and not wearing through, and when you store it in its plastic bag, don't squeeze it in tightly enough to bend or dislocate any links. If the chain is very fine, it may tangle and knot; if this is a problem, wind it around a piece of cardboard or even a cotton ball when you store it.

Silver chains will tarnish, and though you don't want antique jewelry to look new, you don't want it to look dirty either. I like simply to wash my chains in soapy water with a bit of ammonia added, and then rinse and dry them off. You can also use special jewelry dip, available at most jewelers for about $1.00 a jar, and at most jewelry supply stores for a bit less. You can rub with a rouge cloth, too, or any silver polishing cloth, but you should probably wash your chains afterward anyway, so that they don't leave marks on your best blouses. *Don't* lacquer them, or do anything else to make them shiny; silver should have a soft, worn patina and a dullish glow to look its best.

I have much more trouble with gold chains than with silver ones, as I have the kind of body chemistry that makes gold leave black marks wherever it touches me. When I wear a heavy gold chain, it leaves a black track on clothes that is hard to wash off. Keeping the chains clean and free of tarnish doesn't help; it's a reaction between the metal and me. My solution is to spray the chain lightly all over with regular hairspray and let it dry before wearing it. This works well, dries quickly, doesn't shine, and will hold for a couple of wearings. One caution: Don't put hairspray on any piece that has pearls, amber, ivory, turquoise, or other soft material that might react with the chemicals and be spoiled.

Gold chains can be worn together in varying lengths, in combinations of gold and silver (this looks very rich and effective), looped or long, and with all kinds of lockets, pendants, and dingle-dangles as part of the arrangement. Watch chains can sometimes be worn as chokers (if they don't choke you too tightly), and two or three watch chains can sometimes be combined into one very effective long, showy chain. It's good to have a few small chains of various lengths with spring rings or swivels at each end for lengthening short chains. Wear the good-looking chain in front, and the less attractive one in back under your collar, where it doesn't show.

When you wear chains with lockets, pendants, and the like, it is elegant to match the colors of gold (which can vary greatly and need not bear any relationship at all to the karat) and to give thought to the size of the locket in relationship to the heaviness of the chain, and the height at which you want it to hang. Victorian lockets generally hung quite high on the chest, just below the hollow of the throat, but with our modern styles they often look better hanging lower (and that might require that you add a bit of temporary length to your chain). If a locket hangs too low, it tends to bank up against things when you bend over; this can dent or scratch it, so be careful. Watches, especially, are a problem. If they hang too high you can't read them (if you're over thirty!), and if they hang too low they are in danger of hitting against everything. As originally worn (by ladies), they were generally snapped onto the end of a long chain and then tucked into a belt or a watch pocket at the waist. Another way to wear them was to pin them to the blouse front on a special watch pin. Sometimes they were both pinned and attached to a chain, which then swagged handsomely across the bosom. Many beautiful old watch chains of double length have slides, little double cylinders of gold and stones that ride up and down freely on the chain. The proper way to put on a watch chain with a slide is this: Hang the chain over your head with the swivel (where the watch will attach) down. Now pull the chain up from the back of the neck, twist it once, bring it forward over your head and down to the swivel. Then snap the swivel onto the chain where you're holding it. You now have two lengths of chain around your neck. Snap the watch onto the swivel, too, pull the slide up to a central position so that it makes the chain "ray out" nicely, and you're all set!

An old watch chain normally does not have a spring-ring closure, or any closure at all. Sometimes such a chain was cut, a piece of chaining was taken out to be used for another purpose, and a spring-ring closure was added. This harms the integrity of the chain, in my view, and it should not be done.

A long chain should be able to loop over your head and be worn double without difficulty. If you want to triple it, try using a small brooch to clasp two of the strands, pulling the third one to choker length at the throat.

Chapter Nine

Glossary of Antique Jewelry Terms

AGATE. A variety of quartz, agate takes many forms. Some of the most commonly seen in antique jewelry are: banded or striped agate; moss agate (with treelike markings); eye agate (banded agate cut so that the bands form concentric circles, like a bull's-eye; sard (brown); onyx (black); and carnelian (red). Agate is quite hard and, although it will chip, it doesn't scratch easily. It has been used for seals, beads, and decoration since earliest times, and can be beautifully cut into intaglios or cameos. It is easily distinguished from glass by its hardness, weight, and coldness to the touch. Agates mined in Scotland were very popular in Victorian times; today most gem agates are mined in Brazil or in India.

Agates were, and still are, often dyed to intensify their color. Almost all dark-colored agates have been treated. Nineteenth-century black agate was dyed this way: the clean dry stone was immersed in a honey and water or sugar and water solution and kept at a temperature just below boiling for two or three weeks. Then the stones were placed in another pot with sulfuric acid. The honey or sugar absorbed in the first process was carbonized by the acid, and turned black. The stones were then cut, polished, and rubbed with oil to improve their luster. Yellow agates were treated with hydrochloric acid; blue

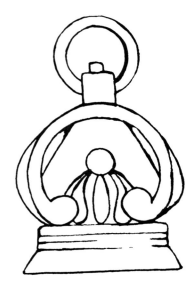

13. **Agate seal**

ones (never found in nature), with potassium ferrocyanide and ferrous sulfate. These blue stones were similar in appearance to lapis lazuli and are sometimes called "false lapis"; real lapis, however, has a different luster and color and is softer than agate. Apple green agate has been dyed with chromic acid. Red agate is dyed with iron vitriol, but red carnelian *does* occur naturally as well.

Agates are noncrystalline (do not occur in crystal form), have a hardness on the Mohs' scale (see HARDNESS) of about 7, and have no cleavage—that is, when they break they do not split along characteristic planes, but have a conchoidal (shell-shaped) fracture, as glass does.

AIGRETTE. A feather-shaped brooch or ornament popular in the eighteenth and nineteenth centuries. It was often set with jewels, or diamonds, and was quite large and imposing. Sometimes the aigrette was a feather holder, worn on a hat or in the hair itself.

A-JOUR SETTING. A cutout setting, usually found on better jewelry, that leaves the back of the stone open "to the day." You will also hear the term used this way: "This setting has been à-joured."

ALASKA DIAMOND. No diamond at all, but rock crystal.

ALBERT. Queen Victoria's husband. Also a style of watch chain named after him, worn in the nineteenth century by both men and women. It generally had a lapel bar on one end and a swivel on the other, with a place in between to hang a charm. The female version, shorter and with more charms, was sometimes called a *Victoria chain.*

ALEXANDRITE. A gemstone discovered in Russia in 1830, on Czar Alexander II's birthday, and named after him. It has the unusual property of looking green in daylight and red under electric lights. (Some less valuable alexandrites change from darker green to brownish-red, and there are many synthetic imitations on the market.) True alexandrites are rare and valuable and must be skillfully cut to bring out their magical play of color.

ALLOY. A mixture of two or more metals. Some commonly known alloys are sterling silver (silver and copper), nickel silver (copper, nickel, and zinc), pewter (tin, copper, and antimony), and pinchbeck (copper and zinc). All gold used in jewelry (unless it is marked 24 karat) is alloyed.

ALMANDINE GARNET. A deep purplish-red garnet, very popular in Victorian jewelry. Almandines are mined in India, Ceylon, Central and South America, and the United States, and the finest of them approach the ruby in color and luster. They are softer than rubies, however, and not as brilliant. They can be distinguished from rubies, too, by placing both under the black light: the ruby glows. Almandine garnets cut *en cabochon* (sometimes with the back hollowed out for greater brilliance) are called "carbuncles." In ancient times these were believed to have magical properties.

AMBER. The fossilized resin of extinct trees, amber is most often found washed up on the shores of the Baltic countries; it is also mined in that area. Amber is light enough to float in water, and it is warm to the touch. It has the unusual (but not unique) property of being easily electrified so that it will pick up tiny bits of paper if it is first rubbed on wool or human hair; this helps to identify it. Amber is usually yellowish, reddish, or brownish in color, though it can also be blue, green, orange, white, or even black. It can be translucent or opaque and is often a mixture of the two. Because it is in fact ancient tree sap, it may hold in its depths bits of vegetation or even tiny insects; these inclusions are highly prized by some amber lovers, particularly Eastern European ones.

Amber has been used for jewelry since ancient times. It was particularly popular in the late nineteenth and early twentieth centuries, when long strands of amber beads were all the rage. Cherry ambers, butterscotch ambers, and tawny or sherry ambers were everybody's favorite "costume" jewelry. They were even thought to be protection against diseases of the throat and lungs.

Amber is unharmed by water or alcohol, but is attacked by acids and should never be in contact with them. In high heat, amber melts—with a characteristic resinous odor that our grandmas believed was antiseptic and medicinal. (It isn't.) This characteristic resinous odor can be recognized when the amber is warmed by friction, or when a tiny bit is filed close to your nose. Plastics and glass, sometimes used to imitate amber, do not smell this way. But *ambroid* (pressed powdered amber) does, and has all the other qualities of amber except that it is not formed naturally, is never clear or combined cloudy-and-clear, and never has the natural inclusions real amber may contain. *Copal,* a resinous yellow opaque material, is often called amber these days, but it is not. Old celluloid was often molded to look like amber, too. This *"ambre antique"* has more clearly defined stripes than natural amber does, and when scraped with a file gives off an acrid or camphorous smell; it is barely electric and highly flammable. Amber, in contrast, burns very slowly.

Another difference: celluloid or plastic can be pared with a knife; amber will not pare—it powders. Most amber is fluorescent under a black light.

Old amber beads were cut in six major styles (many of them in Germany): olives (elongated elliptical beads); *zotten* (cylindrical, slightly rounded, almost flat at the two ends); *grecken* (like *zotten,* but shorter); round; corals (faceted); and horse corals (flat clear beads faceted at the two ends). You will see all these styles represented in old strings of amber beads.

AMETHYST. A purple quartz gemstone, amethyst has been valued for its beauty since ancient times. It is *dichroic*—that is, fine stones show fiery twin colors: bluish purple and reddish purple. Amethyst was a popular Victorian gemstone, and many necklaces, rings, bracelets, and earrings survive. Sometimes amethysts were carved and set with tiny diamonds or gold engraved flowers, or circled with seed pearls.

Amethyst was thought to have magical properties in ancient times, and was believed to cure drunkenness! It is the birthstone for February. Most amethyst these days comes from Brazil, although quite a bit is to be found in the United States: in Maine, Pennsylvania, North Carolina, Georgia, and New Jersey.

AQUAMARINE. A clear bluish or yellowish green gem of the beryl family. The best color is sky blue, but this color is rarely found naturally; most blue aquamarines have been heat-treated.

ARIZONA RUBY. A misleading name for garnets.

ARKANSAS DIAMOND. Another name for rock crystal.

ARMENIAN STONE. Lapis lazuli.

ART NOUVEAU. A romantic "handcraft" movement in jewelry that began in the 1890s and lasted until around 1910. It was a reaction against the "vulgarity" and machined quality of much nineteenth-century jewelry, concentrating instead on graceful, curving, asymmetrical forms, the beauty inherent in natural mottling and "flaws," and unusual and surprising combinations of materials and techniques. Dragonflies, vines, peacocks, flowers, dreamlike faces and figures, moons, and moonlike stones (moonstones, opals, pearls), and metals (silver) were popular; stones with inclusions, irregularly shaped baroque pearls, the natural mottlings of tortoise or horn—all these were interesting to the Art Nouveau designers. So was enameling of all kinds—especially, and characteristically, *plique-à-jour* (translucent enamel, almost like stained glass)—and iridescence of all kinds and in all materials—from peacock feathers to opals to opalescent glass. In fact, this interest in iridescence, rooted in the Art Nouveau movement, has continued as an important design element in jewelry, especially American jewelry, to the present day.

The Art Nouveau movement seems to have started in England, growing out of the earlier Pre-Raphaelite movement, and with roots in Japanese art and Celtic, Renaissance, Gothic, and baroque forms. It soon spread to France, Germany, and the United States, and Art Nouveau jewelry from each of these countries has a basic similarity but special attributes of its own.

Art Nouveau jewelry is in great vogue today and is widely reproduced. Be sure, when buying it, that you are indeed buying original work and not a "repro.'" Many of the repros being sold today are hand finished and carefully cast in molds made from genuine old pieces.

Some of the great names associated with Art Nouveau work are C. R. Ashbee in England; René Lalique, Georges Fouquet, and Henri Vever in France; Georg Jensen in Denmark; and Louis Comfort Tiffany in America.

AVENTURINE. A kind of quartz spangled with bits of mica. Green aventurine is used most often in jewelry. *Aventurine glass* is glass (often used in beads) made to look like aventurine quartz.

BAGUETTE. A gem, usually small, cut in the shape of a narrow rectangle. Diamond baguettes often are used to set off a solitaire in modern engagement rings.

BALAS RUBY. Not a ruby at all, but a red spinel. One of the "rubies" in the crown jewels of England was discovered to be a balas ruby.

BALL CATCH. A modern safety catch, invented around 1911. Basically it is a nearly round C with a small tab that, when pushed into place, completes the circle and holds the pin of the brooch closed.

BANGLE. A round or oval bracelet, rigid rather than flexible.

BAROQUES. Gemstones or beads, especially pearls, of irregular shape.

BELCHER SETTING. A heavy, pronged ring setting, popular around the turn of the century (see Illustration 9).

BERLIN IRON. Early in the nineteenth century, beautiful *cast-iron jewelry* was made in Germany (often inscribed *"Gold gab ich für Eisen"*—"I gave gold for iron").

Patriotic German women had indeed given their gold to help finance the War of Liberation against Napoleon, and got Berlin iron jewelry in return. The vogue for black iron jewelry died out before the middle of the century, and little of it remains.

Berlin iron jewelry, if you find it, will probably be both expensive and beautiful. It is delicate, with whorls or mesh filigree of fine iron wire, or slim chains holding cameolike plaques together. It is neither heavy nor clumsy and is eagerly sought after by collectors.

14.   Baroque pearls

BERYL. A gemstone family with some famous members: emerald (grass green), aquamarine (blue-green), and heliodor or golden beryl (yellow). Beryl is slightly harder than quartz and strongly dichroic (showing two shades of the same color).

BEZEL. The round collar into which a gemstone is set, or the facets on the top of a gemstone.

BIRTHSTONES. Over the ages, different stones have been mentioned as "birthstones": gems that are particularly appropriate—and magical—for those born under certain zodiacal signs or in certain months. Nowadays, these birthstones are generally accepted:
    JANUARY—garnet
    FEBRUARY—amethyst or onyx
    MARCH—aquamarine or bloodstone

APRIL—diamond or rock crystal
MAY—emerald or chrysoprase
JUNE—pearl or moonstone
JULY—ruby or carnelian
AUGUST—peridot or sardonyx
SEPTEMBER—sapphire or lapis lazuli
OCTOBER—opal or tourmaline
NOVEMBER—topaz or citrine
DECEMBER—turquoise or blue zircon

BIWA PEARLS. Lovely lustrous freshwater cultured pearls (often in rice shapes or baroques) that come from Lake Biwa in Japan.

BLACK AMBER. An inaccurate term for *jet.*

BLACK LIGHT. An ultraviolet lamp, useful for identifying some minerals. Long or short wave ultraviolet light excites luminescence or fluorescence in some gemstones (rubies, pearls, opals) and nearly all natural materials (ivory, turquoise, amber), which helps identify them.

BLOODSTONE. Dark green chalcedony sprinkled with red spots, like blood. In ancient times, it was believed that bloodstone stopped bleeding. The Victorians liked it for seals, seal rings, and watch fobs. It is also called *blood jasper, oriental jasper,* and *heliotrope.*

BLUE WHITE DIAMOND. A term used to describe the color of a very fine diamond—not a scientific term at all, but a popular one.

BOG OAK. A peatlike material used and loved by the Victorians, and especially the Irish, for inexpensive jewelry. Bog oak is dark brownish in color and can be distinguished from *gutta-percha,* which is similar to it in appearance, by the fact that it was carved and not molded. Irish bog oak jewelry characteristically shows a castle, a harp, or a shamrock (sometimes all three) as part of the design. Usually the fittings are inexpensive brass, but sometimes they are gold. You will probably not confuse bog oak with jet; jet is lighter in weight, dead black in color, takes a high polish, and—when you rub it on your hair or a woolen sweater—may be weakly electric.

Bog oak jewelry enjoyed its greatest vogue in Great Britain in the first half of the nineteenth century. It is *old* (See Illustration 4.)

BOHEMIAN GARNET. Red or pyrope garnet. Also, sometimes called *Bohemian ruby,* perhaps because these were the favorite stones in inexpensive Bohemian jewelry.

BONE. Jewelry and beads of bone have been used since ancient times, and many nineteenth-century carved pins and beads made of bone are still around—often masquerading as "ivory." But bone and ivory are quite different in appearance. Bone is white or yellowish white, hard, and dull in appearance unless it has been waxed or otherwise treated. If it is grained, the grain-ing is straight—blackish or grayish lines or dots. The material carves dryly, with points and angular lines predominating. When it ages, it yellows. Bone is often stained (sometimes with tea) to simulate the patina of ivory, but the effect is quite different. Ivory (meaning the best real elephant ivory taken from recently killed elephants, rather than ivory taken from long-dead ele-phants or fossil creatures, like mammoths) is glossy and "fat" looking. It is creamy white, with brownish *crosshatched* graining, and as it ages it develops a distinctive beige patina, which is very desirable. It carves even better than bone, but the carving looks quite different—there are glossy polished surfaces, and ivory lends itself to curved lines and softly finished round forms.

If you take the trouble to examine a piece carefully, or—better still—inspect it with your loupe, you should never mistake bone for ivory.

BOULTON, MATTHEW (1728–1809). An important manufacturer of Bir-mingham cut steel jewelry.

BOX SETTING. A square metal setting that enclosed the gemstone like a box, with the edges carefully flattened over the top to hold the stone in place.

BRASS. An alloy of copper and zinc sometimes used in jewelry. When you test for gold, if the nitric acid turns green on contact with the metal, your "gold" is brass. (This reaction of brass to acid is the explanation for the old wiseacre saying: "Take back your ring; my finger's turning green!")

BRAZILIAN EMERALD. Not an emerald at all; a green tourmaline.

BRILLIANT CUT. Modern style of faceting a diamond (or other gemstone) with 58 facets. This takes full advantage of the stone's ability to refract light and appear "brilliant."

BRIOLETTE. A diamond or other gemstone cut into a drop or pear shape.

BRISTOL DIAMOND. Just another name for rock crystal.

CABOCHON. A stone cut in convex form, polished but not faceted. All ancient gems were cabochon cut; faceting did not appear until the Middle

15.   **Ring with cabochon stone**

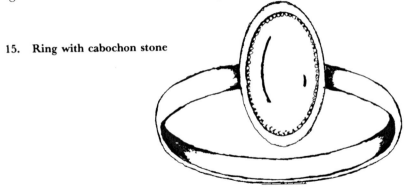

Ages. Cabochon stones were popular in the nineteenth century (particularly garnets), and some stones are nearly always cabochon cut, like agates, turquoise, moonstones, cat's-eye, and "star" gems of all kinds. Art Nouveau jewelry, too, features many cabochon gems.

CAIRNGORM. Yellow or smoky brown clear quartz found in Scotland and featured in old Scottish jewelry. In the nineteenth century it was mined in the Cairngorm Mountains in Scotland, but now those mines are exhausted and real cairngorms are hard to come by.

CALIFORNIA JADE. Not jade; a mineral of the idocrase family called californite.

CAMEO. A stone or shell on which a design is carved in relief. The technique goes back to ancient times, and in the eighteenth and nineteenth centuries, when the ancients were rediscovered and re-revered, cameo cutting and cameo wearing were all the rage. Old cameos were reset, new cameos were made to imitate old cameos, and new cameo styles were originated.

Other materials used for cameos were glass (the work of a famous eighteenth-century imitator of antique cameos, James Tassie, is now collected in its own right) and Wedgwood. Hard stone cameo cutting is almost a lost art today, though shell cameos are still being imported, as they were in the nineteenth century, from skilled Italian cutters.

CANARY DIAMOND. Diamond with a yellow color.

CARAT. English spelling of *karat,* a unit of weight for precious stones and pearls. One carat equals 200 milligrams.

CARBUNCLE. A cabochon garnet.

CARNELIAN. Red or reddish agate.

CASTELLANI. The surname of three nineteenth-century jewelers, a father and his two sons, whose work in reviving ancient styles and techniques greatly influenced Victorian jewelry. The father, Fortunato Pio Castellani (1793–1865), a jeweler in Rome, was fascinated by the archaeological discoveries of his time, particularly gold Etruscan jewelry. He tried to learn the secret of Etruscan *granulation*—a technique in which tiny dots or balls of gold are soldered invisibly to the body of the piece to form a "bloomed" surface. Castellani brought peasant craftsmen who still remembered old techniques from remote Umbria to Rome, and trained them to make "Italian archaeological jewelry"—not reproductions meant to fool customers, but brilliant and beautifully crafted pieces embodying what Castellani knew of ancient styles and techniques. They were immensely popular with English tourists visiting Italy, and soon the style found its way all over Europe, and—like other popular ideas—was often cheapened and exploited by less talented jewelers.

Castellani's two sons, Augusto and Alessandro, continued the family business. Jewelry made by this talented family is often illustrated in books, but rarely—very rarely—offered on the market. If it is, it is bought up at astronomical prices by wealthy collectors. But Etruscan-style jewelry of the period is widely available, and it is often very beautiful and worth owning.

CASTING. A process in which a *model* is reproduced by pouring the casting medium (in jewelry, it would be liquid metal) into a *mold* fashioned from the original. When the mold is removed, or broken, a new piece formed like the original has been made.

Cast jewelry has a different appearance from hand-wrought jewelry. Often the gold or silver shows mold marks—places where the parts of the mold met, and the metal spread a little. These marks may be filed away or finished off, but unless the work was done very carefully, they can be detected by using your loupe. Further, the texture of cast metal is different from that of hand-worked metal. Often air bubbles are present, and the surface of the metal (again, under the loupe) looks "spongier" and less "finished." Careful hand finishing can make both look very similar, but often this much time and care are not expended on cast pieces, which are usually cheaper in price than comparable handmade ones. A handmade piece always shows a certain amount of irregularity: two motifs will never be exactly the same, lines may be slightly irregular, and engraving does not look mechanical but has a more personalized, individual look. Sometimes cast pieces are hand finished, but they still are never quite the same in appearance. Look on the unseen sides of pieces—the inside of rings, the backs of pins and bracelets; handmade ones will usually be finished on the backs as well as the fronts, with motifs carried through fully. Cast ones may be just shells or have plain flat backs. Cast pieces lack a certain sharpness of definition, too; cut-in designs are "soft" rather than sharp and distinct.

Casting alone does not mean a piece is new: it has been practiced for a long, long time. But *machine* casting (often marked by careless finishing, but absolutely uniform repetitions of motifs) is new or nearly new. In general, a handwrought piece has more personality and is more individualized and more valuable than a cast piece of comparable design and quality.

CAT'S-EYE. A yellowish brown chrysoberyl that shows *chatoyancy,* a play of light that appears to move as the stone (cut *en cabochon*) is moved. The late Victorians were fond of cat's-eye and other chatoyant stones (like moonstones, star sapphires, and rubies) as ring stones.

CHALCEDONY. Sometimes used as a synonym for agate, chalcedony is more correctly a nonbanded, noncrystalline quartz stone. It may be marked in various ways, in cloudlike patterns, dotted patterns (like bloodstone), or wavelike patterns. It comes in many colors and can be readily dyed.

CHASING. A technique of working metal (in jewelry, primarily gold or silver) in which the metal is laid on a bed of pitch or a block of wood and worked from the front, with hammer and punches. Chasing is often used to finish a piece after it has been worked up from the back by using another technique: *repoussé. Embossing* is another term for "chasing."

CHATELAINE. A clasp or hook from which was hung all manner of household items: watches, thimbles, scissors, keys, charms, and the like. The word *chatelaine* (from the French) means "mistress of the castle," and the earliest chatelaines were certainly useful for such a person to hang with her important keys, seals, and implements. From the seventeenth century onward, the chatelaine became more and more decorative and whimsical. Eighteenth-century chatelaines were magnificent and elaborate. Cheaper "antique" chatelaines were popular in steel in the last half of the nineteenth century, but by the turn of the century, the vogue was over. The word *chatelaine* is also used to mean the hook plus its pendants.

16. Chatelaine hook

Front View

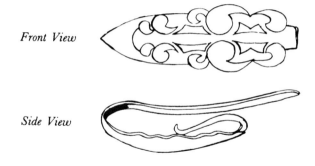

Side View

CHATHAM EMERALDS. Synthetic emeralds developed by Carrol Chatham in San Francisco, California, in 1935. They have the same structure as naturally formed stones, but are more blue-green in color, characteristically tend to have black spots and wispy veillike inclusions, and—under the black light—fluoresce red in the long wave and yellow-orange to olive green in the short wave beam. Natural (and far more expensive) emeralds do not fluoresce, or at best show a very dull, dark response; so a black light will easily distinguish a Chatham emerald from the real thing.

CHATOYANCY. The play of light, like a cat's-eye, in any gemstone. Another term for this is *schiller*. Chatoyant stones (cat's-eye, moonstone, and so on) are always cut as cabochons.

CHOKER. A necklace just long enough to circle the throat.

CHRYSOBERYL. Gem family popular in Victorian times. Some of the members of the family are cat's-eye, alexandrite, and gem chrysoberyl (an asparagus-green clear stone sometimes wrongly called "olivine").

CHRYSOPRASE. Apple-green dyed chalcedony.

CITRINE. Clear yellow quartz. Citrine is *not* topaz, a much rarer, more expensive gemstone. Most citrine used in jewelry is treated amethyst, which turns yellow at high temperatures.

CLAW SETTING. A gem setting (usually used in rings) that holds the stone securely between prongs. The setting allows light to enter the back of the stone, and nearly all large diamonds are set this way. Tiffany settings and belcher settings are types of claw settings. The style became popular in the nineteenth century.

COLLET. Another term for "bezel." A round collar of metal that holds a gemstone in place.

COLORADO JADE. Not jade at all; aventurine.

COPAL. A resinous cloudy-yellow amberlike substance, often sold as amber. It is not.

CORAL. The calcareous skeleton of the coral polyp. Polished and carved coral was highly prized for Victorian jewelry. The coral industry was, and is, centered in Italy, and most gem coral comes from there. In the nineteenth century the favorite colors were salmon red and pale pink (angel skin). Coral was carved into cameos, flowers and fruits, and beads of all shapes. Faceted coral beads usually date from the early part of the century.

Coral is relatively soft (hardness: 3½); it can be easily scratched with a knife blade. When a bit of weak acid (like lemon juice) is droppedi on coral it *effervesces,* this will not happen on plastic or glass imitations.

Coral was often worn by children and was believed to guard them from all manner of diseases and disasters. It was also believed that coral deepened and paled with its wearer's menstrual cycle.

CORNELIAN. Carnelian.

CORNISH DIAMOND. Another term for rock crystal.

CORUNDUM. A famous gemstone family; among its members are sapphire and ruby. It is one of the hardest minerals (hardness: 9), second only to diamonds.

CREOLE EARRINGS. Crescent-shaped earrings, with a wider bottom than top. They were very popular around the middle of the nineteenth century.

CROWN. The top part of a cut gemstone; the portion above the girdle.

CRYSTALS. Rock crystal beads or clear glass beads faceted to resemble rock crystal; crystals are also the orderly form some minerals take when formed in nature.

CULET. The small facet cut on the base of some brilliant-cut or old mine-cut diamonds.

CULTURED PEARLS. Pearls that are formed in the oyster, but induced by man. A small grain of foreign substance is introduced into the oyster. *Nacre,* an iridescent shell-like substance, forms around the grain to protect the oyster; instead, it is his downfall—in a few years people will come looking for the pearl, and usually they find it.

This process was originated and patented by a Japanese noodle peddler, Kokichi Mikimoto, in 1896, and it made him a billionaire. (See chapter seven.)

All pearls, cultured and oriental (natural), will fluoresce under black light (as will some fake pearls made with fish scales); so this is no test either. Still, for all the difficulty in distinguishing cultured from natural pearls, the natural ones are worth many times the price of cultured ones.

CUSHION CUT. A brilliant-cut diamond or other gem that is square shaped with rounded corners.

CUT STEEL JEWELRY. Jewelry set with cut steel faceted "gems" was popular during the eighteenth century as a substitute for diamonds and was often beautifully made, each "gem" carefully cut and studded by hand. In the nineteenth century, cut steel jewelry was already on the decline, and the high standards of workmanship gave way to cheap slapdash costume jewelry—now a substitute for humbler marcasite. But *early* cut steel is beautiful, highly collectible, and very wearable.

DAMASCENING. The art of producing a "watered" pattern in steel, or of decorating metal with inlays of gold and silver.

DELTA PEARLS. Imitation pearls.

DEMANTOID GARNETS. Green garnets, very rarely found today, but used in Victorian jewelry. The color ranges from emerald green to brownish or yellowish green (the most commonly seen). Demantoids are softer than other garnets, softer even than quartz, and unlike other garnets, are attacked and even decomposed by acids. They have a brilliant luster and more "sparkle" than other types of garnet. Demantoids, which come from the Ural Mountains of Russia, are sometimes seen in Russian jewelry, either as cabochons or faceted. If you locate one and can buy it reasonably, you have a find.

DIAMOND. Diamonds need no definition, since they are probably the best known and most popular gemstone of all. It is interesting to note that diamonds are the *hardest* precious stone, defining the top limit of the hardness scale at 10. They do, however, crack, chip, and break even though they don't scratch, and so they must be handled with a certain amount of care. The value of a diamond lies in its size, color, and freedom from flaws. Generally speaking, a two-carat diamond of comparable quality is worth much more than two one-carat stones. Diamonds of very fine color are sometimes called *blue-white* or, more correctly, *of the first water.* Other colors do occur naturally (or are induced by heat treating), and these are called *fancy;* they include pink, yellow, green, and brown. The famous Hope Diamond is a magnificent blue.

Large diamonds are easy to distinguish from other stones. In modern cuts they have a brilliance, a rainbow play of colors, that no other stone approaches. Although zircons, white spinels, and white sapphires have sparkle, the fiery flash of a brilliant-cut diamond is unique. The best of the "counterfeit" diamonds—and there are a number of them—do not really look like the genuine article. Small stones, however, or old-style cuts do not have as much flash, and can be mistaken for other things (or vice versa).

The earliest diamonds we know of appear in Roman jewelry, and they are uncut and not very beautiful. The real glory of diamonds began to be appreciated in the sixteenth century, when the *rose cut* was developed. This is a dome-shaped cut, with a flat bottom and triangular facets that come to a point on top. These "roses" are watery gray in appearance, but beautiful and appealing—they were loved and worn throughout the nineteenth century; but with the invention of the *brilliant cut* around 1700 (generally credited to a Venetian named Vincento Perruzzi), the hidden fire of the diamond was released. Since then, it has been the most desired of gemstones. The eighteenth century is often called the Age of Diamonds, since so much jewelry featured diamonds (or diamond imitations) in pavé settings, presenting a solid sumptuous face to the world.

Nowadays most diamonds are brilliant cut (with 58 or more facets) to show the most fire. Large diamonds of good color are often *square* or *step* cut. But the earlier *old mine cut*—cushion shaped, with a larger table and somewhat fewer facets—is fiery and splendid, too. On the whole, brilliant cut, old mine cut, and rose cut, in that order, are most desirable in terms of price. All other things being equal, the cheapest gem diamonds are *chips,* very small diamonds that are not cut at all, but simply broken up along their natural lines of cleavage.

In ancient times, diamonds were believed to cure poisoning and protect their wearers from the plagues and pestilences that scourged Europe. This latter claim was strengthened by the fact that the plagues first attacked the poorer classes and spared the rich, who could afford diamonds! When diamonds were in contact with the skin, they were also supposed to protect the wearer from nightmares. The diamond is the birthstone for April.

Diamonds were also a symbol of purity and truth, a guard against the Evil Eye, but their power was said to be lost if they were purchased by their owner. Perhaps this was the myth that bred our modern custom of giving diamonds as love gifts. Giving a diamond engagement ring became popular around the end of the nineteenth century; before that, betrothal rings often bore love motifs: two hands holding a heart, clasped hands that opened into two rings (called a *gemel* ring, or a *fede* ring), and *posy* rings with love sayings engraved or enameled on them.

DICHROIC. Showing two shades of the same color.

DOG COLLAR. A high, broad choker, usually made of many strands of pearls, gems, or beads, that completely encircles the neck. The dog collar was all the rage in the last decade of the nineteenth century.

DOUBLET. A stone consisting of two (or more; in that case triplet, quadruplet, or whatever) layers of material glued together, of which only the top layer is gemstone. An opal doublet, for instance, consists of a very thin layer of opal cemented to a cheaper material, perhaps onyx or even glass. If a doublet is sold as a doublet, there's no harm done; but if it is sold as a genuine stone, it is a fraud—and fraud is usually the intention. Needless to say, a doublet is not worth anywhere near the price of a genuine stone.

EILAT STONE. A blue-green stone that is mined near Eilat in Israel. It is a mixture of copper minerals and is said to come from King Solomon's mines.

ELECTROPLATING. A process by which a thin layer of gold or silver is deposited on an object by means of a metal current run through an acid bath. The process was developed around 1830, but not used extensively until around 1860. It is not really satisfactory for putting a gold layer on jewelry because an electroplated layer will soon wear off. Gold filled or rolled gold jewelry will wear far better than an electroplated piece.

ELECTRUM. A naturally occurring mixture of gold and silver, electrum was mentioned by the ancients. Nowadays, we call more or less the same alloy *white gold.*

ELITE PEARLS. Another name for imitation pearls.

EMBOSSING. See *Chasing.*

EMERALD. A beryl of a fine, special color, a velvety emerald green or grass green. The best emeralds are strongly *dichroic,* showing two greens as you look at them: yellow green and bluish green.

Of all precious stones, a really fine emerald of good size is the rarest, since emeralds tend to have inclusions, flaws, unevenness of color, and other peculiarities. A large emerald of good quality, therefore, is worth more in dollars than a diamond of comparable quality.

Because fine emeralds are so rare, you must be especially cautious about what seems to be a "good buy" in an emerald. Make sure (especially if the back of the setting is closed) that is not a doublet or triplet, that it is not green glass, or paste, or demantoid garnet (wonderful in itself, but *not* emerald), or "oriental emerald" (green corundum), green tourmaline, a Chatham (or synthetic) emerald, or even a "soudé emerald" (two layers of colorless quartz or spinel with green coloring between them).

Good emeralds are nearly always square or step cut; in fact, this cut is named for them ("emerald cut"). They have been valued since Cleopatra's times, but the location of the Egyptian mines was lost during the Middle Ages and only rediscovered in 1818. Nowadays, the best emeralds come from South America, principally Colombia, but they are also mined in Russia (since 1830), India (since 1943), Brazil, and in a few other countries.

Emeralds, the birthstone for May, have considerable folklore associated with them, too. They were believed to reveal the unfaithfulness of a lover by changing their color, to heal human eye diseases, and to blind serpents! They were the enemy of enchantment, and so sorcerers could not weave their spells if an emerald was around. Set under the tongue, however, an emerald was supposed to help one predict the future. An emerald was said to strengthen the memory and sharpen the wits, but it was an enemy of passion. Legend tells of a king who, when he embraced his wife with his emerald on his finger, cracked the stone into three parts.

The Victorians do not seem to have been as fond of emeralds as of some other stones, and they are more rarely to be found in nineteenth-century jewelry than, say, the ruby, sapphire, or diamond.

ENAMELING. The art of enameling jewelry has an ancient and brilliant history. It began centuries before the birth of Christ, and has continued—going through the in-and-out-of-vogue phases that all the arts are prone to—until the present day.

The process is one of fusing powdered glass colored with various minerals, by heating it until it glows, and then cooling it. A layer of glass is deposited, which is afterward finished, ground, and polished. Usually the enamel is deposited onto a metal—gold, silver, or copper—but in one kind of enameling technique, *plique à jour*, it is actually suspended between metal strips so that it becomes, literally, stained glass.

In *cloisonné enameling*, thin strips of metal are soldered to the base, and the enamel is flowed into the "cells" that are formed. (*Cloison* means "cell.") *Plique à jour* is like cloisonné, except that there is no base; the enamel is suspended between the strips of metal. This type of enameling was particularly popular with, and characteristic of, the Art Nouveau movement. When you hold *plique à jour* up to the light, it looks like stained glass. *Champlevé* enamel differs from cloisonné in that the cells are dug out of the metal rather than constructed on it. *Basse-taille* is similar to *champlevé*, with this added note: the base is chased with a relief design so that when the enamel flows into the cell and hardens, it is of differing depths. *Painted* or *Limoges enamel* is generally made in this way: a white enamel background is first applied and fired onto a copper plate. Then the picture or design is painted in colors on the background. The piece may be fired several times to get the proper depth of color. *Grisaille* is a similar technique using only blacks, whites, and grays.

Enameled jewelry was very popular in the Renaissance, lost ground somewhat in the seventeenth century, and practically disappeared in the eighteenth century (Age of Diamonds), except for Limoges paintings and portraits. In the nineteenth century, with the renewed interest in the Renaissance, enameling grew popular again; it continued to intrigue jewelry lovers through the Art Nouveau period. Perhaps the most famous enamel jewelry made during this period was the Renaissance-style jewelry of Carlo Giuliano and the fabulous work of Carl Fabergé.

ENGRAVING. Incising or carving a linear design with a sharp tool. Engraving gold and silver is mostly done by machine now, but the hand engraving on old pieces is much more beautiful and individual. Engraving gems, intaglios, and seals has a long and honorable history, but is practically a lost art now.

ETCHING. Cutting designs or patterns into metal (or other material) with the use of acid.

ETRUSCAN JEWELRY. The Etruscans were pre-Romans who ruled Tuscany about eight centuries before Christ. Their gold jewelry was distinctive for its granulation—a technique in which tiny balls or grains of gold were invisibly soldered to the gold background. In the early nineteenth century, when archaeologists uncovered lost Etruscan treasures, Etruscan-style jewelry became the rage, mostly through the work of Fortunato Pio Castellani, a Roman jeweler who designed magnificent pieces based on Etruscan goldwork.

FABERGE. Peter Carl Fabergé (1846–1920) was a goldsmith of French descent who lived in Russia and designed personal fantasy pieces and jewels for the czar and his court. Fabergé's creations were made in his workshops, presided over by master craftsmen; they were impeccably done, with magnificent enameling and perfectly chosen stones. Gems, enameling, and colored golds were all subordinate to the design as a whole. Fabergé pieces are almost impossible to buy nowadays, but pictures of them, along with the occasional exhibits in museums, will give you some idea of the perfection they represented.

FACET. One of the small, flat surfaces cut onto a gemstone.

FANCY DIAMOND. A diamond tinged with color, such as yellow or pink.

FEDE RING. A ring with two hands clasped. This clasped-hands motif goes as far back as Roman days and has been used for love rings since earliest times. The word *fede* means faith, or faithfulness. Sometimes the hands come apart to show a heart or locket or inscription beneath them. When the fede opens into two rings, attached or separate, it is also a *gemel* ring (from the word for twins).

FIBULA. An ancient brooch shaped rather like a safety pin.

FILIGREE. Delicate gold- or silverwork made of fine wire twisted into scrolls or patterning.

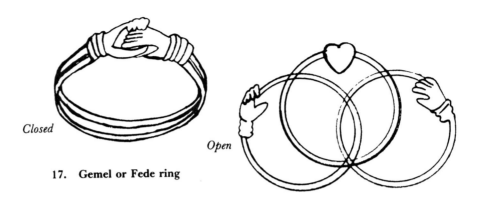

17. Gemel or Fede ring

FOB. A small trinket, pendant, locket, or seal worn to decorate a watch chain. Also used for the watch chain bar, which slipped through a man's buttonhole and held the chain in place.

FOILING. A thin metal backing placed behind a gemstone to deepen or change its color or increase its brilliance. Nearly all stones were foiled ("assisted with foil") before the nineteenth century, and some still are. Nowadays, with more sophisticated faceting techniques, we prefer to set stones *à jour*, so that light can shine through them and so that we can tell exactly what is in the setting. Foiling, however, by no means should be considered a ruse to hide the flaws in a stone. It was and still is a respectable and admired art—as long as it is not used to "cosmeticize" a stone of little value so that it can be sold as a great beauty. Foiled stones should not be cleaned in jewelry dips or exposed to water, as the foils may discolor.

FOOL'S GOLD. Iron pyrites, which has no relationship to gold whatever.

FOUQUET, GEORGES (1862–1929). A widely respected French jeweler of the Art Nouveau period. Alphonse Mucha designed some spectacular pieces for Fouquet.

FRACTURE. The characteristic way a stone *breaks*. Many stones can be identified by their fracture.

FRESHWATER PEARLS. These lustrous pearls come from river mussels rather than ocean oysters. They were much admired by the Victorians, who especially liked the ones that came from Scotland. Today's Japanese Biwa pearls are beautiful freshwater treasures.

FROMENT-MEURICE, F. G. (1802–1855). A French jeweler whose distinctive Gothic jewelry was much admired around the middle of the nineteenth century.

GARNET. A family of minerals that includes almandine garnet (purplish-red), demantoid (green), pyrope (blood red), spessartite (brownish or yellowish red), and grossular (orange or brownish).

Garnets occur widely throughout the world (even in New York's Central Park!) and are generously used in jewelry. Although many stones are very beautiful, garnet is a bit of a stepchild, perhaps just because it is so plentiful. Garnet is not dichroic (does not show two shades of color), and this helps in its identification. It does not fluoresce under the black light, either, and these two qualities help to distinguish it from the ruby, which it sometimes closely resembles. (So-called "Cape rubies" are in fact garnets.)

The Victorians were fond of garnets, and enjoyed them set in both silver and gold; their favorite varieties were pyrope (or "Bohemian") and almandine garnets, with demantoids much admired but more rare. The other varieties are scarcely ever seen. Garnets are often cabochon cut; the pyropes are called carbuncles when they are used this way. The ancients believed garnets would curb bleeding and calm anger and discord. Garnets are the birthstone for January.

GEMEL RING. A ring that separates into two. The word comes from the same root as Gemini: twins.

GENEVA RUBIES. Reconstructed rubies (made by fusing many small bits of ruby together), which appeared on the market around 1880.

GILT. A piece made of another metal very thinly covered with gold. In jewelry, sometimes, you will find a piece that is *silver gilt*, silver beneath a thin coating of gold.

GIRANDOLE. A style of earring or brooch (popular in the eighteenth century) in which three pearl-shaped stones or drops hung down from a larger piece (often shaped like a bow).

GIRDLE. The widest part of a faceted gemstone, the part that is gripped by the setting.

GIULIANO. A family of Neapolitan jewelers who emigrated to London in the 1860s and became famous for their beautiful Renaissance-style jewelry encrusted with enameling like the ancient originals. They also made Etruscan-style jewelry (influenced by Castellani) and Art Nouveau pieces. The father Carlo's mark, CG intertwined, identifies his pieces, but you are not likely to be lucky enough to have one offered to you; most are in museums now or in private collections.

GOLD. It hardly seems necessary here to define gold; and karat, marking, and related terms have been discussed elsewhere. It is interesting, however, to note that gold has been loved and valued since the beginning of time. It was in large measure responsible for the discovery and development of much of the New World, and has started and ended wars and love affairs. In Ben Jonson's

Volpone, the quintessential miser's first words are: "Good morrow to the sun—and next, my gold!" and many people would secretly agree. Gold discovered in California "won" the West and dispossessed the Indians.

GOLDSTONE. Aventurine glass, spangled with bits of metal or mica.

GOTHIC STYLE JEWELRY. In the nineteenth century, sparked by the renewal of interest in the Middle Ages, jewelers designed "Gothic" pieces. One of the famous exponents of this style in France was Froment-Meurice. The pieces were characterized by pointed arches, forlorn maidens, rosette-shaped motifs, castles, and the like.

GRANULATION. Attaching tiny beads or grains of gold to a gold background, without apparent solder. (See Etruscan-style jewelry.)

GUARD CHAIN. A long gold or silver chain worn in the first half of the nineteenth century, to hold a watch or other valuable object. In the 1920s, the new-fangled wristwatch replaced the guard chain, the watch chain, and the watch pin, and they became all but extinct.

GUNMETAL. A bluish-black metal popular in Edwardian jewelry. It is an alloy of copper and tin.

GYPSY SETTING. A ring setting in which the stone is sunk to the surface of the gold, with rays cut around it in a starlike pattern. This style was popular in the late nineteenth century.

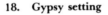

18. Gypsy setting

HAIR JEWELRY. Whole books could be written on the subject of hair jewelry—pieces primarily composed of, or featuring, the hair of a beloved person. The fashion for hair jewelry began in the sixteenth century, when memorial rings and pendants composed of hair as a background for gold initials of the deceased (all set under carved crystal) began to make their appearance. Hair jewelry became extremely popular in England around 1800 and continued in vogue for the next 75 years. During this time, hair rings with braided hair set into gold, or with inside hair compartments; hair bracelets of braided hair set with gold or hair clasps; brooches with pictures artfully made out of bits or tresses of hair; hair "lockets"; earrings and necklaces made of "beads" of woven hair; and hair watch chains and charms—all were popular.

Not every piece of hair jewelry was a *memento mori*. Many a hair locket held the tresses of a romantic "flame" or a beloved parent or child. Queen Victoria's sixteenth birthday present from her mother was a brooch made from that lady's own hair.

Often a woman made her own hair jewelry, aided perhaps by an instruction book or directions printed in her favorite magazine. A complete set of hair tools could be bought: a china palette to lay the hair on, pencils, curling iron, a table of glass to form the groundwork of a hair picture, knives, scissors, gum, goldbeaters' skin (the membrane of the large intestine of an ox, used in the process of separating gold into very thin leaves), gold wire, India ink, and watercolors; all these were mentioned as aides. In one contemporary account (an 1870s publication, *Cassell's Household Guide*), the directions first specify that the hair should "undergo a thorough purifying" with hot water, washing soda, and borax, then be spread out on a palette and scraped with a knife edge, and finally rewashed in borax. Directions for braiding or plaiting hair called for strips of it to be attached with gum to goldbeaters' skin, neatly woven and pasted onto a paper backing, pressed, then cut into shape for insertion in a locket.

More elaborate designs were suggested: hearts, bay wreaths, stars, and family trees, with hair from every member of the family. The gray hair of the grandparents was suggested for the trunk, and the downy hair of the smallest babies for the outermost leaves.

Pictures made of hair, often assisted with ink painting or drawing, were popular too. A favorite design was "The Prince's Feather," a love motif rather than a memorial one. A more somber pattern, though equally popular, was "Tomb-and-Willow," which usually portrayed a sad female figure leaning against a willow tree that drooped mournfully over a grave. Gummed hair had to be cunningly cut, curled, and manipulated to form these pictures, which were often further adorned with bands of paper, ink or pencil drawing, gold wire, or tiny pearls. (This is not so different, in my mind, from the fine hand-beading of flowers, dried flower pictures, or delicate découpage that so many women find absorbing today.)

If a woman was not inclined—or skilled enough—to make her own hair keepsake, she could send the hair of her beloved to a jeweler, or to a specialist like Simonson's Human Hair Emporium in New York City; their catalog advertised various styles of gold fittings for hair:

> The beautiful custom of keeping remembrance of our dear departed
> ones in Photographs, or Souvenirs, originated the idea of enclosing locks

of hair in Ornamental Cases, and this gave rise to the prevailing fashion of Hair Jewelry; which is indeed most desirable as a keepsake. Our pattern book represents 1450 . . . Different Styles of Ornaments, of artistic workmanship. . . . Perfect satisfaction guaranteed both to the Designs and the use of the hair intrusted to us.

This last was not an unnecessary promise; it was rumored that some unscrupulous houses simply threw away the hair "intrusted" to them and used the already prepared hair they had on hand!

Hair jewelry was enormously popular in England, France, and the United States. During the Civil War, countless husbands, wives, and sweethearts exchanged hair jewelry, and many of the surviving American pieces date from that period. A few decades later, as the century drew to a close, hair jewelry declined, too; it has never made a "comeback."

HALLMARKS. Marks stamped with tiny punches on gold and silver jewelry (and other objects), usually to indicate correct karat of gold and/or the payment of a tax. English marks include the mark of the assay office (which tells the city where the piece was made), the date letter (which indicates the year in which it was marked), the karat, and sometimes a maker's mark or other special marks. American jewelry is often unmarked, but many countries demand that all gold and silver be marked, and most jewelry made for export must be marked. A small book telling how to read silver or gold marks (they are substantially the same) can be bought inexpensively in most good bookstores. Learning to read the marks on your jewelry, if any are there, is an indispensable part of truly knowing your pieces.

HANDKERCHIEF RING. Occasionally you will find a small gold ring attached by a chain to a larger one (often octagonal). This is a handkerchief ring—a popular whimsy in the 1870s.

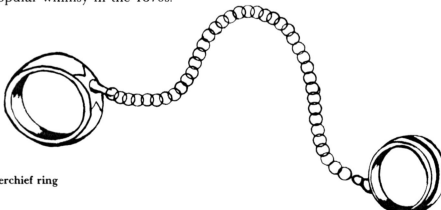

19. **Handkerchief ring**

HARDNESS. One of the ways of identifying gemstones is by their hardness, or their ability to resist scratching. The Mohs' scale of hardness, which was developed in 1822, is standard:

1. Talc	6. Feldspar
2. Gypsum	7. Quartz
3. Calcite	8. Topaz
4. Fluorspar	9. Corundum
5. Apatite	10. Diamond

Each mineral in this list can scratch all the ones above it. "Hardness points" can be purchased at a jewelry supply store; they are needles with marked hardness, for testing. Obviously, with jewelry, you do not want to scratch a gem in a way that will spoil it, in order to identify it. However, if you can find an inconspicuous spot, or use the gem in question to scratch something else less hard, you may be able to accomplish your purpose.

A less scientific, but very useful, hardness scale is my own homely version. Herewith the Goldemberg scale:

fingernail — 2½	glass — 5½
copper penny — 3	steel file — 6–7
knife blade — 5½	

A note of caution: *hardness* is not the same as *toughness* (the ability to withstand breakage). Objects that are extremely hard may shatter easily, so don't drop your diamonds!

HERKIMER DIAMOND. Rock crystal found in Herkimer County, New York.

HESSONITE. Grossular garnet.

HOOP RING. A ring in which stones are set side by side, to form a hoop. Early in the nineteenth century this kind of ring was sometimes given as a promise or betrothal ring, especially a hoop ring of pearls.

HOPE SAPPHIRE. A complete misnomer for synthetic blue spinels.

HSIU YEN. Green and white jasper; *not* jade.

HYACINTH. Hyacinth or jacinth is mentioned in the Bible. Today "hyacinth" is yellowish or orange zircon or garnet, but since the Greek root of the word means "blue," it may also have been a sapphire the ancients meant to describe.

IMPERIAL JADE. Jade of the finest luminous emerald green color.

IMPERIAL MEXICAN JADE. A cheap imitation; green-dyed calcite.

INCLUSION. Foreign material—gas, liquid, or mineral—enclosed in a gemstone.

INLAY. To set one material into the body of another so that the surface is level. For example, *piqué* is tortoise *inlaid* with gold and silver.

INTAGLIO. Gemstone or other material into which a design is cut. A seal is an intaglio.

IVORY. Ivory should mean "elephant ivory," the tusks of recently killed Indian or African elephants. However, the term is sometimes used to denote different "ivories": *fossil ivory* (the tusk of the extinct woolly mammoth); *hippopatamus ivory; walrus ivory; whale ivory; vegetable ivory* (the nut of the ivory palm tree, the doum palm, and other similar trees); or even *"French ivory"* (plastic). Real elephant ivory has characteristic brownish crosshatched graining, and is more beautiful and more costly than the others. Bone is the most usual lookalike for ivory (see *Bone*). A test for *vegetable ivory*: drop a bit of sulfuric acid onto the piece; if it turns pink, it's vegetable ivory.

JADE. Jade or *yu* is the most precious Chinese stone, more beloved in the Orient then either diamonds or gold. It is actually *two* minerals, nephrite and jadeite, which are similar but by no means the same. Nephrite has been carved in China for thirty centuries; any jade that is sold to you as ancient should be nephrite jade. Jadeite was discovered in Burma only a few hundred years ago, but is generally the more highly regarded stone in Europe and America today. Both jadeite and nephrite are extremely *tough* minerals, though their hardness ranges only from 6½ to 7. The most desirable color for jadeite is translucent emerald green (imperial jade), but greenish or white with deep green spots (moss on snow) is very valuable, too, as are pink, tangerine rind, white (mutton fat), or bluish jade. Much of the value of jade lies in its exquisite carving, as well as its color and translucence. The mineral is so resistant that skilled jade carvers may have taken years to complete a small piece you can hold in your hand.

Prices on jade have climbed recently (as what has not?) and, in view of the many imitations and look-alike minerals on the market, you should be certain of what you are buying before you spend a large amount on jade. Bowenite (a variety of serpentine) is sometimes called "New Jade." It is being imported now as a jade substitute, often beautifully carved, but it can be scratched with your fingernail or a piece of glass. It is not jade.

Other common jade imitations are prehnite, californite, saussurite, and just plain glass. Jade is warmer than most stones to the touch, but colder and heavier than glass; it has a distinctive musical click when two pieces are struck together.

Jade was very popular in good Art Deco jewelry, and quite a bit of it is around today as we renew and rewarm our relationships with mainland China. But be careful; all that is sold as jade *isn't.*

JASPER. Absolutely opaque qaurtz stone of dark color. Jasper is distinguished from chalcedony in this way: if no slightest fragment of the stone is translucent, it is jasper; if any edge shows translucency, it is chalcedony. Jasper is usually dyed dark red, brown, green, or yellow.

JENSEN, GEORG. A Danish silversmith who designed distinctive jewelry and tableware. His shop was founded in Copenhagen in 1904, and the firm still does business all over the world. Early signed Jensen pieces are valuable collector's items.

JET. A variety of fossil coal, very dense and homogeneous, with a perfect conchoidal fracture. Jet is a fine lustrous black in color, absolutely opaque; it has a hardness of only 3 to 4. It feels warm to the touch and usually is slightly electric; when you rub it on your hair or a woolen sweater it will sometimes pick up tiny bits of paper. It is often called black amber, but it is not amber; it is darker, heavier in weight, takes a higher polish, has a less "waxy" feel, and is less electric than true amber.

The best jet came from the mines in Whitby, England, and was used for mourning jewelry during the nineteenth century. Shortly after the turn of the century, the popularity of mourning jewelry declined, the mines closed down, and the skilled jet carvers disappeared.

French jet is not jet, but glass—heavier, colder, harder, and more brittle. Black onyx, which is stone, is much heavier and harder than jet, much colder to the touch, and much more brilliant in its luster.

Jet was never expensive jewelry, but some of the carving on it was very fine. If you come across it, and like it, buy it; it is truly old, of the period, not being made anymore—and is bound to skyrocket in value as the years go by.

JEWELER'S TOPAZ. Citrine.

JUMP RINGS. Small round O-shaped connecting rings for necklaces, charm bracelets, and other pieces. They can be bought in silver, gold, or base metal from jewelry supply stores.

20. Jump ring

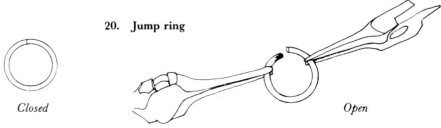

Closed   *Open*

KARAT. A term used to define the fineness of gold. *Fine gold,* or pure gold, is 24 karat; 18 karat, or 18k, is 75 percent gold and 25 percent alloy; and so on.

KEEPER RING. A ring worn to prevent the loss of another ring, or two rings that serve to bracket a valuable ring (such as a wedding or engagement ring). In the nineteenth century, chased gold *keepers* were often worn to protect a plain gold wedding ring. Another term for a keeper is *guard ring.*

KOREA JADE. Bowenite, a common, cheaper substitute for jade.

KUNZITE. A beautiful and rare violet-colored stone discovered in California around the turn of the century.

KYANITE. A rare blue stone that sometimes resembles sapphire. It is mined in a number of Asian countries and in North Carolina.

LACE BROOCHES (OR PINS). Very small, delicate brooches worn around the turn of the century. They were often bought and worn in twos and threes.

LAKE GEORGE DIAMOND. Another name for Herkimer Diamonds— rock crystals.

LALIQUE, RENE (1860–1945). Perhaps the most famous of the Art Nouveau jewelers, Lalique won fame in Paris of the 1890s when he made a spectacular group of jewelry for the great actress Sarah Bernhardt. He innovated the use of a nude female on jewelry (widely copied thereafter), and loved new combinations of materials, fantastic dreamlike beasts and insects, and brilliant color. Later, around 1910, he abandoned jewelry for glass, and became even more famous and innovative in this medium.

Lalique pieces today are rarely to be seen outside museums and picturebooks, but they are spectacular. Don't miss a chance to meet one if you have the opportunity.

LAPIDARY. A specialist in working in gemstones other than diamonds.

LAPIS LAZULI. A beautiful deep blue mineral known and loved since ancient times. The Egyptians treasured its color and magical properties and used it as a cure against melancholy. Lapis is a rather soft stone (hardness 5½–6), which never takes a glassy polish. It has an uneven fracture and rarely crystallizes; therefore, its appearance is more like the massy, soft look of turquoise (though the color is quite different) than that of any of the other gemstones. Always absolutely opaque, it has markings of different kinds, sometimes various shades of blue and blue-black, sometimes white veining, sometimes brassy flecks of iron pyrites (called gold by those who don't know).

Glass imitations of lapis are sold, but the color is never as intense as the true stone, and on the smallest broken surface, you can tell the bright conchoidal fracture of glass from the dull uneven fracture of lapis. Dyed agate, too, is much heavier, shinier, and different in color from true lapis; *azurite*, sometimes sold as lapis, is also much heavier as well as softer than the true stone.

When lapis is touched with hydrochloric acid, it loses its color and gives off a strong smell of hydrogen sulfide (rotten eggs); this, however, is a fatal test and only to be performed with great care and on an absolutely unseen area. Light blue lapis is sometimes heat-treated to form the more desirable dark blue color; the color change is permanent.

LAVA JEWELRY. In the middle decades of the nineteenth century, wealthy Britons and Americans took the "grand tour" of Europe and stopped at Pompeii to see the ruins. They often brought home skillfully carved cameos made from the lava and set into brooches, necklaces, bracelets, and parures, usually mounted in gold. These lava cameos are fairly easy to buy, and are often quite beautiful, ranging in color from cream to dark brown, and usually showing "classical" women's faces.

LIMOGES ENAMEL. See *Enameling*.

LOCKET. A pendant that opens up to reveal a picture or memento inside. Lockets containing a miniature of the beloved were a popular nineteenth-century engagement gift. Men wore them as watch fobs, and women and girls wore them at their throats. Sometimes hair lockets containing mementos of dead or living loved ones were used as clasps for bracelets or were hidden in the backs of memorial rings. During the 1870s, a large heavy locket of silver or gold was a fashion necessity; portraits of women of the period nearly always show them wearing such a locket high on their chests, with its own heavy chain or velvet ribbon. Children, too, wore tiny gold heart-shaped or round lockets. Most old lockets had small frames with rock crystal, glass, or celluloid to protect the enclosure; these should still be in the piece if it is in "mint" condition.

LOST WAX CASTING. See *Casting*.

LOUPE. A jeweler's magnifying glass, worn in or close to the eye. A 4x or 5x loupe is sufficient for most jewelry study; a 10x loupe is better for examining stones. A "hand loupe" is a small, powerful magnifying glass that fits into its own metal case.

LOVE STONE. Aventurine quartz.

LUCITE. A kind of clear plastic; modern.

MACHINE STAMPING. A cheap way of making jewelry, machine stamping, was first used around the middle of the nineteenth century, but it was not until about 1870 that machine stamping "took over" and the great bulk of inexpensive jewelry was routinely made this way. A machine-stamped piece is never as desirable as a comparable handmade piece of jewelry.

MADEIRA TOPAZ. Citrine.

MALACHITE. An opaque copper mineral marked with characteristic bright and darker bands of green. Malachite has a hardness of only 4, and is always cut cabochon, flat, or in beads (never faceted). The ancients valued it as a talisman for children, and it was often hung in a cradle to protect the tiny occupant. It was believed to be especially powerful if it was engraved with a picture of the sun.

Much malachite was mined in the Ural Mountains of Russia, and artists like Fabergé carved beautiful decorative dishes and animals out of this fascinating stone. In the early decades of the nineteenth century, malachite jewelry enjoyed a vogue in England, and beautiful gold parures were set with malachite. In the 1870s, when Scotch agate jewelry was so fashionable, malachite was sometimes set into silver bracelets and pins with the same styling as the agate ones.

If a drop of hydrochloric acid is dropped on malachite, it will *fizz;* if you do this, watch carefully with a loupe and quickly wipe the acid off as soon as you see a reaction. You will not harm your stone.

MANCHURIAN JADE. Not jade at all, but soapstone.

MARCASITE. The stones we call marcasite in jewelry are really iron pyrites, better known as "fool's gold." They occur very widely in nature, and have been used for jewelry as far back as the ancient Greeks. In the eighteenth century, marcasite was very popular, beautifully mounted in silver and adorning lockets, brooches, and various other pieces. By the nineteenth century, marcasite had been relegated to cheap costume jewelry, in which it was often glued rather than set. There was a brief vogue for marcasite set in sterling in the Art Deco period, and these pieces are being collected again now.

Marcasite is sometimes confused with cut steel, which it resembles. Cut steel, however, was bolted onto backplates. Turn your piece over, and if you see tiny pegs behind each stone, they are not marcasite but cut steel.

MARQUISE. A stone or setting with the shape of a pointed oval, or "boat." A marquise diamond is a beautiful variation of the brilliant cut; it has been popular for the last two or three decades as an engagement stone. The marquise setting, often used for eighteenth-century memorial rings, continued to be popular in the nineteenth century.

MEMENTO MORI. Latin for "Remember you must die." A term for memorial jewelry.

MEMORIAL JEWELRY. Jewelry that commemorated the death of a loved one or of a famous person. Memorial rings were often commissioned by the family of the deceased and given to friends or to those who attended the funeral. Hair jewelry was sometimes memorial jewelry, as was jet jewelry, black onyx, and enameled jewelry that bore the name and death date of the remembered, or perhaps a phrase like "In Memoriam," or "Remembered." Memorial motifs included the "Tomb-and-Willow," forget-me-nots, angels, skulls and skeletons, urns, tombs, and broken columns. White enameling generally signified a dead child or unmarried girl or boy; black enameling was standard for adults. Twin black bracelets of jet or other black beads were worn as "mourning bracelets." Often memorial jewelry was inscribed and dated—a great help to the collector!

The custom of wearing memorial jewelry "died out" in the last decades of the nineteenth century.

MEXICAN JADE. Green-dyed calcite.

MILLEGRAIN SETTING. A nineteenth-century setting in which the stone is held by many tiny grains or beads of gold.

MIZPAH. This word, which means "The Lord watch between me and thee, when we are absent one from another," was a favorite sentimental watchword on lover's jewelry in the last decades of the nineteenth century. Mizpah rings and pins were especially popular.

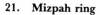

21. Mizpah ring

MOHS' SCALE. See *Hardness.*

MOONSTONE. A colorless, almost transparent feldspar that shows a milky sheen, or chatoyancy, in reflected light. The bluer the sheen, the finer the moonstone. Moonstones are always cut *en cabochon* or in round balls. In the late nineteenth century, when colored stones were "out," moonstones (often in combination with diamonds and pearls) were all the rage.

Moonstones are fairly soft (hardness: 6) and easily scratched. The moonstone is a sacred stone in India; it has long been treasured as a gift for lovers, one that arouses passion and bestows the power to read the future. Most moonstones come from Ceylon.

MOSAIC. The same nineteenth-century travelers who brought home lava cameos and coral jewelry from Italy were likely to favor mosaics as well— jewelry on which a picture or pattern was made up of tiny bits of stone or colored glass.

Florentine or *pietra dura* mosaic was made of pieces of cut stone (coral, malachite, turquoise, for examples), usually in a flower pattern, cemented into black marble. *Roman mosaic* was made of colored glass set into a black glass surround; it usually pictured ancient monuments, birds in nests, spaniels, and the like. The best of the Roman mosaics were so fine that they looked like paintings. Sometimes the backs or surrounds of the Roman mosaics were of goldstone, and most often they were mounted in gold.

Mosaics are still quite easy to buy and reasonable in price, but be careful—when you check them out—that all the original pieces are in place and that there are no chips or cracks anywhere.

Roman mosaics are still made in Italy and Greece. Make sure, if you buy an antique mosaic piece, that it is *old* and not contemporary.

MOSS AGATE. See *Agate*.

MOTHER-OF-PEARL. The nacreous inner shell of mollusks that produce pearls. It has been used for beads, jewelry, and decorative objects since Egyptian times.

MOURNING JEWELRY. Memorial jewelry.

NACRE. The iridescent material secreted by pearl-producing mollusks; the material pearls are made of.

NAVETTE. A boat-shaped stone or setting; another name for a *marquise* cut or setting.

NEPHRITE. See *Jade*.

NEVADA TURQUOISE. Variscite.

NEW JADE. Bowenite, a form of serpentine, often carved and exported from China in imitation of true jade.

NEW ZEALAND GREENSTONE. Dark green nephrite jade from New Zealand.

NICKEL SILVER. Not silver, but an alloy of copper, nickel, and zinc. Another name for it: German silver.

NIGHT EMERALD. Peridot.

NITRIC ACID. A strong acid used to test gold. Like other strong acids it can burn the skin, and should be handled with care.

NOBLE. Used to refer to a gemstone, this term means the same as "precious."

OBSIDIAN. Natural volcanic glass, usually black or gray in color. It sometimes has lace or flower markings, and it has been used in jewelry and other decorative objects. "Apache tears" are obsidian.

OCCIDENTAL. When a stone is called "occidental" anything, it usually means it is a fake or of poor quality. Conversely, "oriental"—as in the case of pearls—often means good or genuine.

OLD MINE CUT. See *Diamonds*.

ONYX. See *Agates*.

OPAL. An oxide of silicon gemstone that is unique for the play of "fire"— little points of many-colored lights—in its interior. Opals have no fracture lines or lines of cleavage, and so they are always cut flat or in cabochons. They range in color from milky white to deep peacock blue (called "black"), and through many blues, greens, and pinks in between. Some opals, almost water-clear, are called *water opals;* they resemble moonstones except for that characteristic flashing "fire."

Opals are fairly soft (hardness: 5½ to 6½) and very fragile. They are easily scratched and very easily chipped and broken. Besides this, they have water trapped in their hearts, and if they are not taken care of properly they "dry out" and "die." Queen Victoria, a practical lady, championed them after they were discovered in Australia in 1839, and she succeeded in making them popular with the Victorians.

Most opals still come from Australia. They are now very much in demand, and are sometimes imitated by opalescent glass—but the two are quite dissimilar. The main caution about opals is to beware of doublets—thin layers of opal cemented to less precious materials and passed off as a single stone. Opals are the birthstone for October.

The ancients believed the opal had a beneficial effect on the eyesight and also could render its wearer invisible. Scholars are not sure how far back in history opals were known, but Shakespeare mentions them in *Twelfth Night*: "Thy mind is a very opal."

OREGON JADE. Green jasper.

ORIENT. The sheen of fine pearls.

ORIENTAL. Usually, when "oriental" is used before the name of a gemstone, it means fine or genuine. Sometimes, however, it means the stone is a kind of sapphire, or a stone from the East. For example, *oriental almandine* is purplish sapphire; *oriental amethyst* is purple sapphire; and *oriental ruby* is a ruby from Burma. *Oriental pearls* are natural, uncultured pearls.

PALLADIUM. A white metal, similar to platinum but lighter in weight and cheaper in price. Like platinum, it does not tarnish and is easily worked. Palladium was known in the nineteenth century, but has not been much used in jewelry until comparatively recent times.

PANAMA PEARLS. Blue or gray pearls from the Gulf of Mexico.

PARIS PEARLS. Imitation pearls.

PARURE. A matching set of jewelry, usually a necklace, brooch, earrings, and bracelet. Parures were popular in the eighteenth and nineteenth centuries, and a great find today is a complete parure in its own original box. *Demi-parures* are smaller sets of jewelry—perhaps just a brooch and earrings, or a necklace and earrings.

PASTE. "Gemstones" made of a special kind of glass. The fine paste jewelry of the eighteenth century was valued for its own beauty and workmanship and was not "imitation" anything. Each beautiful paste was cut, foiled, and set with care, and pastes were worn without apology by kings and queens.

The look of these paste pieces is quite distinctive. The stones were usually set *en pavé*, like a pavement; although they may have been of slightly different sizes, the top surfaces were even, and very little metal showed. They were usually set in silver, and each paste showed a black dot in its center from the way it was foiled and cut.

By 1840, open settings had replaced closed ones, and pastes began to be silvered on the backs of the stones, rather than foiled. This signaled the deterioration of paste jewelry. Nowadays, jewelry set with glass stones is cheap costume and more or less considered worthless. But never turn up your nose at *early* paste pieces; they are avidly collected, rare and often very costly, and can be exquisitely beautiful.

PAVE SETTING. Stones or pastes set "like a pavement," with the top surface even and very little metal showing.

PAVILION. The part of a cut gemstone that is below the girdle.

PEARLS. Certain bivalves secrete a material called nacre. When this material is deposited around a grain of sand or other irritating substance, a pearl is formed. Sometimes the pearl is separate from the shell; sometimes it may form a blister of one shape or another. The most costly pearls are those that are large, of regular round size and fine color. But there is also a considerable market for baroque (irregularly shaped) pearls, colored pearls (which may be brownish, pink, gray, bluish, or even black; natural black pearls are rare and very costly), and flat-backed or Mobe pearls, which are set in rings.

Oriental, or natural, pearls are more valuable than *cultured,* or man-induced, pearls (see *Cultured Pearls*). A strand of well-matched, good-sized oriental pearls of fine color and luster can cost many thousands of dollars.

Pearls should be kept in well-controlled temperature and humidity, since dryness and heat are bad for them. They should be reknotted and cleaned from time to time by a reputable expert. And they should be *worn* as well, since wearing seems to improve their luster. Acids of any kind attack them, so never clean them in ordinary jewelry cleaner, or spray them with cosmetics, hairspray, or perfume.

Pearls have been used as love gifts since earliest times; a pearl hoop ring was a common betrothal present in the nineteenth century. A pearl is the birthstone for June.

Cultured pearls are almost indistinguishable from natural ones, except by using sophisticated instruments. Imitation pearls of any kind—glass, plastic, or other compositions—are quite different in color, luster, weight, and appearance, and should never fool anyone who studies them carefully.

PENNSYLVANIA DIAMOND. Iron pyrites, or "fool's gold."

PERIDOT. The gem variety of the mineral olivine. Peridot (or chrysolite) is a distinctive yellowish green in color (rarely brownish), rather soft (hardness: 6½), and has an oily luster. It was inexpensive and popular in the nineteenth century, particularly in the last decades, and was often used in combination with pearls and diamonds.

In a thirteenth-century book of magical symbols, there is this mention of peridot: "A vulture, if [carved] on a chrysolite, has the power to constrain demons and the winds. . . . The demons obey the wearer."

PICOTITE. Black spinel.

PIETRA DURA. See *Mosaics.*

PIGEON BLOOD RUBY. A ruby of magnificent purplish-red color; the most favored color for rubies.

PIGGYBACK STONE. A kind of doublet.

PINCHBECK. In the early eighteenth century, a London watchmaker named Christopher Pinchbeck invented an alloy of copper and zinc that looked and acted like gold. It did not tarnish, wore well, and could be worked easily. He, and his sons after him, used this secret formula to make "gold" jewelry. When the family died, the secret formula died with them.

Other alloys of zinc and copper have been used to make cheap metal jewelry, and in modern times these are usually gold plated and called *gilding metal*. True Pinchbeck is rare and sought after. Many dealers will call anything that is gold-colored metal "pinchbeck," but this is a misuse of the term.

PIQUE. As early as the seventeenth century, Huguenot craftsmen in England were producing handmade piqué jewelry—tortoiseshell inlaid with gold and silver. Some of these early pieces were exquisitely ornate, with several colors of gold and elaborate designs of flowers and leaves. The metal was inlaid in the tortoise by melting a channel for it with a hot tool. As the century wore on, piqué work was done by machine, and these later versions were less detailed and usually showed geometric patterns—lines, stars, and balls.

Piqué work is often very beautiful, and as it grows older and rarer it gets more expensive. Only a few years ago tortoise jewelry could be bought for a few dollars; now it has gone up perhaps ten times in price. If you buy it, make sure it is perfect, as in the course of time tortoise may dry out and shrink and the gold and silver may fall out. Ivory inlaid in this way is also called piqué.

PLASMA. A dark green chalcedony, similar to jasper. Plasma with red spots of jasper is called *bloodstone.*

PLASTICS. Plastics have been used in jewelry for much longer than most people realize. Celluloid (a trade name for a pyroxylin and camphor compound) was invented by an American, John Hyatt, in 1868, to simulate ivory, and was used widely in the latter half of the nineteenth century for dental plates, celluloid collars, billiard balls, toilet articles, and small decorative pieces.

Casein plastics (made from milk protein) and Bakelite (developed in 1909 by Leo Hendrik Baekeland) were used widely in the first decade of the twentieth century. Brightly colored phenolic resins came into wide use in the 1930s and are well known to lovers of Art Deco jewelry.

A book could be written on plastics alone—and for those used in old jewelry, at least a few cautions must be noted. All early plastics are quite soft (hardness from about 1½ to 2½) and easily scratched. They are very light in weight and warm to the touch, and many will dissolve in acetone or acids.

Several of the plastics mentioned above have been used to imitate ivory, tortoise, amber, or gemstones. Imitation tortoise gives the most trouble, since natural amber and ivory are readily identifiable (see *Amber* and *Ivory*). The best test is to file the "tortoise" in an inconspicuous place, holding it close to your nostrils as you do , and *sniff*. Tortoise smells like burning hair; plastic smells acrid, like sour milk. Under a microscope, tortoise shows red spots and plastics do not; but the uneven patterning of true tortoise and the more regular, mechanical patterning of plastic will often give it away.

Art Deco plastic jewelry is now being collected for itself, and is rising in price. *If* you like it and can pick it up cheaply enough, it is probably a good investment.

PLATINUM. Although platinum has been known since at least as far back as the sixteenth century, its use for jewelry was limited until the middle of the nineteenth.

Platinum is a bright white metal that never tarnishes and resists the attack of nearly every chemical except *aqua regia* (a mixture of nitric and hydrochloric acids). It is easy to work, "whiter" in look than silver, has an extremely high melting point, shows virtually no wear, and is heavier even than gold (and more expensive).

A few Parisian jewelers made mourning rings out of platinum (the word is derived from the Spanish word for silver: *platin*) as early as 1828, but around the middle of the century Fontenay, a French jeweler, used platinum rather than silver to set diamonds. By the twentieth century, it had nearly replaced silver for this purpose; and by the 1920s, as more platinum became available from Canada and South Africa, the popularity of the metal skyrocketed, especially as a setting for diamond rings.

Platinum is a member of a group of metals that includes palladium, rhodium (in modern use for plating silver), osmium, ruthenium, and iridium. Platinum is generally not marked and can be distinguished from silver and white gold (if you don't have a gold testing kit) by its color, its resistance to wear, and its weight.

PLIQUE A JOUR. See *Enameling*.

PORCELAIN. A fine white high-fired ceramic material sometimes used for portrait or picture paintings.

POSY RINGS. In the fifteenth to eighteenth centuries, rings engraved on the inside with a romantic motto were often used in England as wedding or engagement gifts. The "posies" were, in fact, *poetry* or *poesie:* rhymed statements of love, like "True love hath led my heart to choose/My heart is dead if you refuse." There were also posy lockets.

PRECIOUS. In jewelry, this term is specific. It means—in the case of metals—gold, silver, platinum, and palladium; in the case of gemstones—diamond, ruby, sapphire, and emerald. It does not necessarily imply cost or value.

22.   Posy locket

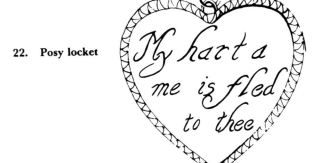

PRESSED AMBER. See *Amber.*

PYROPE GARNET. See *Garnet.*

REGARD RING. In the nineteenth century there was a vogue for rings set with colored stones that spelled out a love word. The most popular were

> R—ruby
> E—emerald
> G—garnet
> A—amethyst
> R—rose diamond
> D—diamond.

DEAREST was also used, and sometimes the stones spelled out a secret word known only to the lovers, or a first name.

If you find a Victorian hoop ring with different-colored stones or a knot ring or other ring with tiny stones of different colors set into it, perhaps you have one of these old charmers.

REPOUSSE WORK. A pattern beaten up from the back of a piece of metal, with the use of hammers and punches. Nearly always, a repoussé piece is also *chased*, or finished from the front, as well.

Repoussé work has been known since earliest times. In the finest and most elaborate work, the pattern is raised so high it looks almost like bas-relief sculpture.

RHINESTONE. A cheap glass stone, used as a poor imitation of a diamond.

RHODIUM. See *Platinum.*

RING GUARD. A small strip of metal, usually gold or gold filled, which is set inside the shank of a ring to make it smaller.

RING GAUGE. A set of rings in different sizes used to tell what your ring size is.

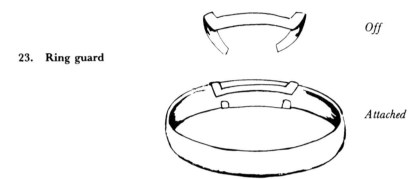

23. **Ring guard**

Off

Attached

RING STICK. A tapering rod of wood or metal used to size and polish rings. Another name for this is *mandrel.*

RIPE PEARL. A pearl with fine luster, or orient.

RIVER PEARL. Freshwater pearl.

RIVIERE. A necklace made from diamonds or other gemstones.

ROCK CRYSTAL. Clear, colorless quartz. The word *crystal* dates back to Greek times and means "ice." Rock crystal has been used for carving seals and, in the eighteenth century, was the stone of choice in most memorial jewelry. Beautiful eighteenth-century rings set with crystal can still occasionally be bought; they are usually curved around the shank and enameled with the remembered person's name, age, and date of birth. In the 1920s "crystal" beads (which were sometimes rock crystal and sometimes glass) were popular, and many of them survive.

Rock crystal is easy to tell from glass. It is heavier, harder, colder, and is doubly refractive—that is, the appearance of the string through the beads (or a pencil line seen through the stone) is doubled.

Rock crystal can also be distinguished from *paste* by some of these characteristics. Further, set pastes generally show a black dot in the center of the stone; rock crystals do not.

Like all quartz, rock crystal is fairly hard and wears quite well. When it is subjected to heat, it develops a bit of "fire," and this property was exploited in the days of the grand rock crystal chandeliers. As the manufacture of glass became more sophisticated, all the clarity and fire of crystal could easily be duplicated in cheaper, lighter glass, and rock crystal was no longer used in this way.

The crystals used for crystal ball gazing as far back as Greek and Roman times were probably of rock crystal; certainly they were in later centuries. This divination with crystal was called *scrying*, and many books were written about it. Rock crystal was also believed to be a symbol of purity and virginity and to have the power to bring rain.

ROLLED GOLD. Another term for "gold filled." See chapter six.

RONDELLE. A flat, disk-shaped bead, usually used as a spacer between more valuable or decorative beads. Sometimes the edges of a rondelle are faceted.

ROSE CUT. See *Diamond*.

ROSEE. A delicate shade of pink, very desirable in pearls.

ROSE QUARTZ. Pink cloudy quartz, sometimes used as a gemstone, as beads, or carved into a seal.

ROUGE CLOTH. A polishing cloth for gold and silver jewelry. It can be bought inexpensively at a jewelry supply store and lasts almost indefinitely.

RUB-OVER SETTING. A closed setting in which the metal is worked up over the rim of the stone and evened out level with it. This setting is often seen in eighteenth-century jewelry.

RUBY. A red corundum gemstone, ruby is a prized, costly, and rare precious gem. The most favored color is "pigeon's blood," a deep purply-red, but the ruby also comes in various shades of pink and scarlet. An interesting fact about its color is that it does not change under artificial light; many other red stones do.

Rubies have been prized and admired since ancient times, but within the last century or so it has been discovered that several famous "rubies" were in reality other kinds of stones. Very large rubies are rare and are worth more, generally speaking, than diamonds of comparable quality. Most rubies are dichroic, showing two shades of red as you study them; this distinguishes them from garnets, for example, which show only a single shade. Rubies are also harder than garnets, which are about 7 on the Mohs' scale; rubies are 9, second only to diamonds (at 10).

Synthetic rubies formed of the same material as natural rubies were developed late in the nineteenth century, and were marketed widely in the first decade of the twentieth. They are different in color from natural rubies, being a rather sharper, "hotter" pink; under the black light, natural rubies glow deep red and synthetics glow more brightly red. If you have the two together, you can easily see the difference.

Most rubies are mined in Burma, Ceylon, and India. A few have been found in this country in North Carolina and Montana.

At one time people believed that a fire shone in the heart of a ruby; if it was placed in a glass of water, the ruby would make the water boil! In the fourteenth century, the ruby was treasured as a bringer of peace and a guardian of lives and lands—but only if it was worn on the left side. The ruby is the birthstone for July.

RUSSIAN CHRYSOLITE. Demantoid garnet.

RUTILATED QUARTZ. Rock crystal with fine needlelike inclusions.

SAPPHIRE. Precious blue corundum gemstone. Like the ruby, it is exceedingly hard and is mined primarily in Siam, Ceylon, Burma, and India. It, too, is dichroic—it shows two shades of blue. But sapphires also occur in other colors, including white (colorless), pink, yellow, brown, and green. The most favored color, and the one most usually associated with sapphire, is deep cornflower blue.

Sapphire is slightly less costly than ruby, which is a bit more rare, and sapphires of other colors than blue are generally much less valuable. White sapphires are often passed off as diamonds, though they have nowhere near the diamond's fire. In the 1930s many women pawned or sold their diamonds and replaced them with white sapphires, which were then called "Depression Diamonds." In the nineteenth century, pink sapphires were quite common.

Ancient references to "sapphire" are now generally thought to have meant lapis lazuli, but the sapphire *was* worn as a symbol of wisdom and was valued as an antidote against poison. Changeable sapphires, which showed blue in some lights, violet in others, were especially valuable and were used to determine (among other things) the chastity of women. Sapphire was also called "eyestone," and believed to be able to cure eye diseases. Sapphires are the birthstone for September.

SARDONYX. Chalcedony with red and white bands, often used for cameo carving.

SARK STONES. Amethyst.

SATIN STONE. Satin spar, a kind of gypsum.

SAUTOIR. A long necklace (sometimes of pearls) with a tassel at the bottom, popular in the last decades of the nineteenth century.

SCARAB. A carved representation of a kind of beetle revered by the ancient

Egyptians as a symbol of life or of rebirth. The flat bottom of the scarab was often carved too, and used as a seal. In the nineteenth century, with the rediscovery of Egyptian treasures, scarabs and representations of scarabs were popular again. And in the 1920s after Tutankhamen's tomb was opened, Egyptian motifs—the scarab in particular—were widely used in jewelry.

SCHILLER. Sheen or play of light in a chatoyant stone, such as a moonstone.

SCIENTIFIC STONE. Glass, or sometimes a synthetic stone.

SCOTCH AGATE JEWELRY. Around the middle of the nineteenth century, Scotch agates of various colors and patterns were set into chased silver (or, less commonly, gold) pins, earrings, bracelets, and (rarely) necklaces (see Illustration 10). The stones were carefully matched, flat or slightly cabochon in cut, and highly polished. Some of the popular motifs were anchors, circles, St. Andrew's crosses, swords in scabbards, butterflies, feathers, love knots, locks and keys, and buckles.

Queen Victoria, who loved her Scottish castle in Balmoral, was also a devotee of Scotch agate jewelry and helped to make it popular. There is still a good bit of it on the market, but the prices have been steadily rising. A good Scotch agate piece set in gold would nowadays bring several hundred dollars; the same piece in silver might go for about a third of that price.

SEMIPRECIOUS STONE. An imprecise term, it generally means any gemstone other than sapphire, ruby, diamond, or emerald.

SHELL CAMEO. The helmet shell (brown and white) and the shell of the giant conch (pink and white) are the most commonly used types for cameo carving. Shell cameos have been popular since the beginning of the nineteenth century, when they were popularized as a cheaper substitute for stone cameos. The tradition of shell cameo cutting goes back at least as far as the fifteenth century. Most shell cameos are cut in Italy, and some are quite fine.

SHOULDERS OF A RING. If the central stone of a ring were its head, the part near the head—in the position of its shoulders—is called "shoulders."

SIGNET RING. A ring with a seal or intaglio carving as its central motif. This carving may be in stone or in the metal itself, and it may represent initials, a crest, or a symbolic design.

SILVER. The commonest of the precious metals. Fine silver is pure silver, which is seldom used for jewelry because it is too soft. Sterling silver is 925 parts of silver to 75 of copper, the alloy most often used. Silver weighs about half as much as gold, has greater reflectivity, but is not as malleable. It has always been less expensive; a comparable piece of gold jewelry might cost four or five times as much as a silver one. The price of silver jewelry follows the price of gold jewelry, however, so as gold rises, silver inevitably does too.

Silver has been used since ancient times, but has not survived as well as ancient gold because it tarnishes and decomposes. There have been times, however, when silver was "in"; we are going through such a vogue today.

Platinum, white gold, palladium, and nickel silver all bear some resemblance to silver, but on close inspection various differences are apparent. Silver is unique in its soft, grayish color and its mellow patina, built up of fine scratches and treasured as evidence of years of careful polishing and wear.

SOLITAIRE DIAMOND. A diamond (usually of fine quality and good size) set by itself, as an engagement ring. This kind of betrothal gift became popular around the end of the nineteenth century.

SOUDE STONES. Doublets.

SOUTH AFRICAN JADE. Not jade at all, but green garnet.

SPANISH EMERALD. Green glass.

SPANISH TOPAZ. Heat-treated quartz.

SPINEL. Mineral family related to corundum. Spinels are only a little less hard than rubies and sapphires (hardness: 8) and are often confused with them. Spinels come in pinks, reds, and blues, and are manufactured synthetically in other colors, notably "white" or clear. Spinels are *not* dichroic like corundum stones, and therefore can be distinguished from them on that basis, but many mistakes are made. Since spinel is far less valuable, if you are in doubt, consult a gemologist.

A red spinel is called a *balas ruby,* and many famous old rubies have turned out, on more informed analysis, to be spinels.

SPRING RING. A round ring with a small knob that opens or unlocks it. A spring ring is most often used, in association with a *jump ring,* as the closure of a necklace or bracelet.

24. **Spring ring**

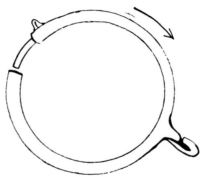

STAR RUBY. A ruby with *asterism*, a star-shaped light reflection caused by fine inclusions in the stone.

STAR SAPPHIRE. A sapphire showing the same *asterism* as a star ruby.

STAUROLITE. A stone that naturally occurs in cruciform crystals. Used as an amulet in some European countries, it has been found in Brittany, Switzerland, Scotland, Russia, Brazil, and the United States. Most often the color is reddish or blackish brown.

STEP CUT. A popular cut for colored gemstones. The table of the stone is cut square, oblong, or in another shape, but the facets around and below it are rectangular.

STERLING. See *Silver.*

STRAPWORK. Flat metal bands or ribbons, usually surrounding a central motif like a frame.

STRASS. A kind of paste invented by Georges Frederic Stras, a Parisian jeweler of the eighteenth century.

SUNSTONE. Goldstone, or aventurine.

SWISS LAPIS. Blue-dyed jasper.

SWIVEL. Egg-shaped connector, found on the ends of watch chains, to which the watch attaches.

25. Swivel

TASSIE, JAMES (1735–99). A maker of fine imitation paste cameos. His work was well regarded in his own time and is avidly collected now (when it can be found).

TIFFANY. A world-famous New York jewelry store, founded by an astute family, one member of which, Louis Comfort Tiffany, was responsible for patenting a unique iridescent glass and introducing Art Nouveau to America. His father, Charles Lewis, founded the firm in 1837 (along with John B. Young) and scored a jewelry coup by going to France and buying up Napoleonic treasures for sale here.

TIFFANY SETTING. A simple high-pronged setting for solitaire stones, introduced by Charles L. Tiffany in 1886.

TIGER'S-EYE. Brown and yellow banded chatoyant quartz.

TOPAZ. Although the word *topaz* is synonymous with a clear sherry color, the topaz gemstone is not always that color at all. In fact, it often occurs as yellow, blue and greenish blue, white (colorless), or rose pink. The sherry topaz comes only from Brazil and is the most sought-after color.

Topaz is hard stone (8), but is easily cracked or fissured internally. These fissures give an iridescent look to the stone, which spoils its appearance. Topaz is easily electrified and (like amber), when it is rubbed on hair or woolen clothing, it will pick up small bits of paper. It is electrified by heating too, and will retain the electricity for more than twenty-four hours.

Topaz is dichroic, showing two shades of color as you turn it. The finest topaz has great life and luster and is a truly beautiful gemstone. Pink topaz, popular in the nineteenth century, occurs naturally but also may come from heat-treated yellow topaz; these pink stones are often foiled to give greater depth to the color.

Many other stones are miscalled topaz. *Oriental topaz* is yellow sapphire; *topaz quartz* is citrine. True topaz is the November birthstone.

TORTOISE. The shell of the hawksbill turtle has been esteemed as a jewelry material since ancient times. The finest color is usually considered to be translucent golden yellow with brown markings. Tortoise has been used for toilet articles, combs and brushes, small boxes, and other *objets d'art* as well as for jewelry. It was often inlaid with silver and gold patterns, a craft the Huguenots brought over from France to England in the seventeenth century. (See *Piqué.*) The tortoiseshell was shaped by steaming, or softened in boiling water and then pressed into molds.

The Victorians were very fond of tortoise and used it enthusiastically. Today, with tortoise an "endangered species," it is little used as a decorative material. Many plastics, however, still ape its mottled richness.

Tortoise has a hardness of about 2½ and ranges in color from deep mottled brown to unmarked orangy yellow (yellow belly). It is always partially, and sometimes wholly, translucent. Distinguishing tortoise from plastic is not always easy (see *Plastics*). Old, dry tortoise pieces can be improved with a long bath in mineral or other oils and a light coat of wax. Since tortoise scratches easily, it may also benefit from polishing, but this should be done only with the greatest of care—and by an expert.

TOUCHSTONE. The hard black stone that precious metals are rubbed on for touchstone testing.

TOURMALINE. A mineral family of strongly dichroic gemstones of many colors: red, pink, blue, white (clear), and green occur regularly. Tourmalines, like topazes, are highly electric and will pick up small bits of paper when rubbed on hair or woolen clothing, or when subjected to heat or pressure.

Tourmaline has a hardness of 7–7½, but it takes a high polish and is a gemstone of considerable beauty. Pink tourmaline was popular in the nineteenth century, as was green; watermelon tourmaline (pink tourmaline surrounded by green) is especially arresting.

Some of the finest tourmaline comes from this country: the mines at Mount Mica (near Paris) and Mount Apatite (near Auburn) in Maine. It is also mined in Russia, Brazil, South Africa, and other countries, and is found in many American localities.

TRAP CUT. Step cut.

TURQUOISE. A blue or blue-green gem mineral, rather soft and porous, turquoise has a hardness of only 6. Like opal, it is subject to many disasters, and must be taken care of if it is to be preserved in all its beauty.

Turquoise tends to absorb dirt from the environment, will sometimes turn greenish or lose color with age, and is easily nicked and scratched. It is also easy to simulate, and glass or plastic turquoise, plastic-impregnated natural stone, or pressed material made from turquoise dust can fool all but the most observant.

The finest color in turquoise is rich sky blue; the least valued is generally green. Turquoise in which the matrix is black and well distributed (like a spiderweb) is highly valued in American Indian jewelry. The size of a stone, too, has to do with its value. Turquoise is always cut flat or in cabochons; since it is completely opaque, it is never faceted.

The finest sky blue turquoise comes from Persia, but many mines in the southwestern part of our country produce strikingly beautiful material.

Ancient Turks (the word *turquoise* comes from the same root as the word *Turkish*) believed that turquoise was a protective talisman for horses, and often hung turquoises on their horses' frontlets. In the sixteenth century, turquoise was believed to be a man's stone and was worn exclusively by men. It was believed also that the stone had magic powers if given as a gift.

The mid-Victorians were fond of turquoise, especially little rounds or cabochons set in rings or pavé set on brooches, bracelets, and necklaces; they were especially effective in combination with gold and diamonds or pearls. Of course our own American Indians revere turquoise and craft it with silver into magnificent (and much copied) jewelry.

Turquoise is the birthstone for December.

VEGETABLE IVORY. See *Ivory.*

VEVER, HENRI (1854–1942). Leading French Art Nouveau designer and author of a famous (and, alas, exceedingly rare) book on nineteenth-century jewelry.

VULCANITE. A hard black rubber substance, similar to gutta-percha, occasionally used in inexpensive jewelry.

WEDGWOOD. The firm of Wedgwood and Bentley, in the eighteenth century, specialized in making porcelain cameos and intaglios. Many of these pieces were set into jewelry, often framed in cut steel, pinchbeck, or—more rarely—gold.

The Wedgwood potteries are still in existence and still making fine, modestly priced porcelain ware. The old pieces are sought after and eagerly collected—and are correspondingly high in price.

WHITE GOLD. An alloy of gold with silver, palladium, platinum, or nickel.

ZIRCON. A fiery stone that usually occurs naturally in a red-brown color; when heat-treated, however, the stones will become blue, yellow, or white (clear). Zircons are softer than diamonds (hardness: 6½–7½) but can look quite a bit like them.

Naturally occurring yellowish-red zircon is called *hyacinth* or *jacinth* and is a beautiful gemstone. Straw-yellow zircons from Ceylon are called *jargoons.* Hyacinths that have been heat-treated to turn white are often mistaken for diamonds. They were used in mourning jewelry in place of diamonds with fair frequency.

Zircons have suffered because of their similarity to diamonds. They are generally considered "cheap" substitutes and looked upon with some disdain. That is a pity because in its own right the zircon, especially hyacinth, is a beautiful and elegant stone.

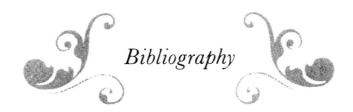

Bibliography

Amaya, Mario. *Art Nouveau.* Studio Vista, 1971.

Anderson, B. W. *Gem Testing.* New York: Emerson Books, Inc., 1948.

Bainbridge, Henry Charles. *Peter Carl Fabergé (Goldsmith & Jeweller To The Russian Imperial Court)* Feltham, Middlesex, England: The Hamlyn Publishing Group, 1966.

Banister, Judith. *English Silver Hall-Marks* Slough, Bucks, England: W. Foulsham & Co., Ltd. 1970.

Barsali, Isa Belli. *Medieval Goldsmith's Work* Feltham, Middlesex, England: The Hamlyn Publishing Group, 1969.

Battke, Heinz. *Ringe Aus Vier Jahrtausenden* Frankfurt, Germany: Insel-Verlag, 1963 (Buckrei).

Bauer, Dr. Max. *Precious Stones* (Vol. I, II). New York: Dover Publications, 1968.

Berliner, Rudolf. *Italian Drawings for Jewelry 1700–1875,* An Introduction to an Exhibition at the Cooper Union Museum for the Arts of Decoration—Sept. 9 through Oct. 19, 1940. John B. Watkins Co.

Blakemore, Kenneth. *The Retail Jeweler's Guide* London, England: Illiffe Books, Ltd., 1969.

Blum, Stella. *Victorian Fashions & Costumes from Harper's Bazaar 1867–1898* New York: Dover Publications, 1974.

Bradford, Ernle. *Four Centuries of European Jewelry* London: Spring Books, 1967.

———. *Victorian Jewelry.* London: Spring Books, 1967.

Bruton, Eric. *Dictionary of Clocks & Watches* New York: Bonanza Books, 1963.

Buck, Ann M. *Victorian Costume & Costume Accessories* New York: Universe Books, 1970.

Burgess, Frederick W. *Antique Jewelry & Trinkets* New York: Tudor Publishing Co., 1972. (Reproduction of 1919 edition)

Burton, Elizabeth. *The Pageant of Georgian England* New York: Charles Scribner's Sons, 1967.

Cellini, Benvenuto. *Treatises on Goldsmithing & Sculpture* Translated by C. R. Ashbee. New York: Dover Publications, Inc., 1967.

Cirdot, J. E. *A Dictionary of Symbols.* New York: Philosophical Library, 1962.

Clifford, Anne. *Cut Steel & Berlin Iron Jewelry.* Bath, England: Adams & Dart, 1971.

Clutton, Cecil, and Daniels, George. *Watches.* New York: The Viking Press, 1965.

Coarelli, Filippo. *Greek & Roman Jewelry* Feltham, Middlesex, England: The Hamlyn Publishing Group, 1966.

Contini, Mila. *Fashion from Ancient Egypt to the Present Day* New York: Crescent Books, 1965.

Cooper, Diana, and Battershire, Norman. *Victorian Sentimental Jewelry* Cranbury, N. J.: A. S. Barnes & Co., 1973.

Cunnington, Phillis. *Costume In Pictures* Studio Vista, 1964.

Curran, Mona. *Collecting Antique Jewelry.* New York: Emerson Books, Inc., 1970.

Dakin, W. J. *Pearls.* New York: Cambridge University Press, 1913.

Darling, Ada. *Antique Jewelry.* New York: Century House, 1953.

———. *Antique Jewelry Identification* Iowa: Mid-America Book Co., 1969.

———. *The Jeweled Trail, Collecting Antique Jewelry.* Iowa: Wallace-Homestead Book Co., 1971.

Detari, Angela Hojj. *Old Hungarian Jewelry* Corvina Press, 1965.

Dickinson, Joan Younger. *The Book of Pearls* New York: Bonanza Books, 1968.

Epstein, Diana. *Buttons.* New York: Walker & Co., 1968.

Evans, Joan. *A History of Jewelry (1100–1870)* Boston: Boston Book & Art Shop, 1970.

Falkiner, Richard. *Investing in Antique Jewelry.* London, Barrie & Jenkins Ltd., 1975.

Fallon, John P. *The Marks of the London Goldsmiths & Silversmiths* New York: Arco Publishing Co., Inc., 1972.

Flower, Margaret. *Jewelry 1837–1901 (Collector's Pieces).* New York: Walker & Co., 1969.

———. *Victorian Jewelry.* Cranbury, N.J.: A. S. Barnes & Co., Inc., 1967.

Foskett, Daphne. *British Portrait Miniatures.* London: Methuen & Co., 1963.

Fregnac, Claude. *Jewelry from the Renaissance to Art Nouveau.* London: Octopus Books, Ltd., 1973.

Garner, Phillipe. *The World of Edwardiana.* Feltham, Middlesex, England: The Hamlyn Publishing Group, 1974.

Gere, Charlotte. *American & European Jewelry (1830–1914).* New York: Crown Publishers, Inc., 1975.

————. *Victorian Jewelry Design.* Chicago: Henry Regnery Co., 1973.

Gerlach, Martin. *Primitive & Folk Jewelry* New York: Dover Publications, Inc., 1971.

Greene, Edward B. *Portrait Miniatures* Ohio: Cleveland Museum of Art, 1951.

Gregorietti, Guido. *Jewelry Through the Ages.* Feltham, Middlesex, England: The Hamlyn Publishing Group, 1969.

Higgins, Reynold. *Jewelry from Classical Lands* London: The Trustees of the British Museum, 1969.

Hinks, Peter. *Jewelry* Feltham, Middlesex, England: The Hamlyn Publishing Group, 1969.

Hoffman, Herbert, and Davidson, Patricia. *Greek Gold, Jewelry from the Age of Alexander.* New York: The Brooklyn Museum, 1965.

Hornung, Clarence P. *A Source Book of Antiques & Jewelry Designs* New York: George Braziller, Inc., 1968.

Hughes, Graham. *Jewelry.* New York: E. P. Dutton & Co., 1966.

Jackson, Sir Charles J. *English Goldsmiths & Their Works.* New York: Dover Publications, 1964.

Janson, Dora Jane. *From Slave to Siren* North Carolina: Duke University Museum of Art, 1971.

Jones, William. *Finger Ring Lore* Singing Tree Press, 1890.

Klein, Dan. *All Color Book of Art Deco.* London: Octopus Books Ltd.

Kornitzer, Louis. *The Jeweled Trail.* New York: Sheridan House, 1941.

Kunciou, Robert. *Mr. Godey's Ladies (Being a Mosaic of Fashions & Fancies).* Princeton, N.J.: The Pyne Press, 1971.

Kunz, George Frederick. *The Curious Lore of Precious Stones.* New York: Dover Publications, 1971.

————. *Rings.* Philadelphia: J. B. Lippincott Co., 1917.

Kurz, Otto. *Fakes.* New York: Dover Publications, Inc., 1967.

Kybalova, Ludmilla; Herbonova, Olga; and Lamarova, Milena. *The Pictorial Encyclopedia of Fashion.* Translated by Claudia Rosoux. New York: Crown Publishers, Inc., 1968.

Lewis, M. D. S. *Antique Paste Jewelry.* Boston: Boston Book & Art Publisher, 1970.

Liddicoat, Richard T., and Copeland, Lawrence. *The Jeweler's Manual.* New York: Gemological Institute of America, 1967.

Loff, Joseph, and Richards, Alison. *The Pleasure of Jewelry & Gemstones* London: Octopus Books, 1975.

Luscomb, Sally C. *The Collector's Encyclopedia of Buttons.* New York: Bonanza Books, 1967.

Mason, Anita. *An Illustrated Dictionary of Jewelry.* Illustrated by Diane Packer. New York: Harper & Row Publishers, 1973.

McClinton, Katharine Morrison. *Antiques of American Childhood.* New York: Clarkson N. Potter, 1970.

Meyer, Florence E. *Pins for Hats & Cravats Worn by Ladies & Gentlemen* Iowa: Wallace Homestead Book Co., 1974.

Milliken, William M. "The Art of the Goldsmith." *Journal of Aesthetics & Art Criticism,* Volume VI., No. 4, June 1948.

Mollett, T. W., *Dictionary of Art & Archaeology.* New York: American Archives of World Art, 1966.

Mourey, Gabriel, and Vallance, Aymer. *Art Nouveau Jewelry & Fans* New York: Dover Publications, Inc., 1973.

———. *European Art Nouveau Jewelry.* New York: Century House.

Nijssen, L. Giltay. *Jewelry* New York: Universe Books, Inc., 1963.

Oman, Charles. *British Rings (800–1914)* London: B. T. Batsford, Ltd., 1974.

Pergolesi, Michelangelo. *Classical Ornament of the 18th Century.* New York: Dover Publications, Inc., 1970.

Peter, Mary. *Collecting Victorian Jewelry* London: MacGibbon & Kee Ltd., 1970.

Peters, R. R.; Kegg, G. M.; and Feiro, T. E. *Antique & Old Jewelry Price Guide.* Astrom Industries, 1971.

Plenderleith, H. J., & Werner, N. E. A. *The Conservation of Antiques & Works of Art.* New York: Oxford University Press, 1956.

Purtell, Joseph. *The Tiffany Touch.* New York: Random House, 1972.

Rose, Augustus, and Cirino, Antonio. *Jewelry Making & Design.* New York: Dover Publications, Inc., 1967.

Sataloff, Joseph. *The Pleasures of Jewelry & Gemstones.* London: Octopus Books, Ltd., 1975.

Savage, George. *The Art & Antique Restorers' Handbook.* New York: Frederick A. Praeger, Inc., 1967.

Singer, Dr. Paul. *Early Chinese Gold & Silver.* China House Gallery, China Institute in America, 1971.

Sinkankas, John. *Van Nostrand's Standard Catalog of Gems* New York: Van Nostrand Reinhold Co., 1968.

Smith, Grace Howard, and Smith, Eugene Randolph. *Watch Keys as Jewelry* Syracuse, N.Y.: Syracuse University, 1967.

Speltz, Alexander. *The Styles of Ornament.* New York: Dover Publications, Inc., 1959.

Vilimkova, Mitada. *Egyptian Jewelry* Feltham, Middlesex, England: The Hamlyn Publishing Group, 1969.

Wills, Geoffrey. *Ivory* Cranbury, N.J.: A. S. Barnes & Co., 1968.

Yates, Raymond F. *Antique Fakes & Their Detection.* New York: Gramercy Publishing Co., 1950.

Catalogs

Baird-North Co.—Diamonds, Watches, Jewelry, Silverware (1913). Iowa: Wallace Homestead Book Co.

Dover Stamping Co., 1869, The American Historical Catalog Collection. Princeton, N.J.: The Pyne Press, 1971.

The Crystal Palace Exhibition Illustrated Catalogue: London, 1851. Art-Journal reproduction of 1851 edition. New York: Dover Publications, Inc., 1970.

Gatter, Robert S. *Catalog & Price List of Diamond, Gold & Plated Jewelry & Silver Things, 1900.* New York: Century House.

Jewelry Fashions (1896 Illustrated Catalogue) Marshall Field & Co. Gun Digest Publishing Co., 1970.

Jewelry Watches & Silver—E. V. Roddin & Co. (1895) Catalog. Princeton, N.J.: The Pyne Press, 1971.

Lord & Taylor—*Clothing & Furnishings.* Princeton, N.J.: The Pyne Press, 1971.

Victorian Shopping: The Harrods Cataloque, 1895. England: David & Charles Reprints, 1972.

Pamphlets and Magazines

The Art of Personal Adornment. New York: Museum of Contemporary Crafts, 1975.

Brooches In Scotland Scotland; The National Museum of Antiquities of Scotland, 1966.

Carroll, Diane Lee. *Ancient Exotic Jewelry.* Newark, N.J.: The Newark Museum, Winter, 1967.

———. *European & American Jewelry of the 19th Century.* Newark, N.J.: The Newark Museum, Spring, 1967.

Crosses. Newark, N.J.: The Newark Museum, Spring, 1960.

The Egyptian Collection of the Cleveland Museum of Art. By Staff of Dept. of Ed. Cleveland, Ohio: The Cleveland Museum of Art.

Laver, James. *Fashion Art and Beauty.* New York: Metropolitan Museum of Art Bulletin, November, 1967.

Legend & Lore About Diamonds & Things. New York: Fortunoff, 1970.

The Metropolitan Museum of Art Bulletin, New York, 1966.

The Metropolitan Museum of Art Bulletin, New York, August/September, 1971.

The Metropolitan Museum of Art, New York, Calendar/News, May/June, 1973.

Poicons d'Or et de Platine, 6M Edition. Paris: Tardy.

Two Centuries of French Fashion New York: The Brooklyn Museum, 1949.

Victorian & Edwardian Decorative Arts London: Her Majesty's Stationery Office, Victoria & Albert Museum, 1952.

Index

141

AUTHORS GUILD BACKINPRINT.COM EDITIONS are fiction and nonfiction works that were originally brought to the reading public by established United States publishers but have fallen out of print. The economics of traditional publishing methods force tens of thousands of works out of print each year, eventually claiming many, if not most, award-winning and one-time best-selling titles. With improvements in print-on-demand technology, authors and their estates, in cooperation with the Authors Guild, are making some of these works available again to readers in quality paperback editions. Authors Guild Backinprint.com Editions may be found at nearly all online bookstores and are also available from traditional booksellers. For further information or to purchase any Backinprint.com title please visit www.backinprint.com.

Except as noted on their copyright pages, Authors Guild Backinprint.com Editions are presented in their original form. Some authors have chosen to revise or update their works with new information. The Authors Guild is not the editor or publisher of these works and is not responsible for any of the content of these editions.

THE AUTHORS GUILD is the nation's largest society of published book authors. Since 1912 it has been the leading writers' advocate for fair compensation, effective copyright protection, and free expression. Further information is available at www.authorsguild.org.

Please direct inquiries about the Authors Guild and Backinprint.com Editions to the Authors Guild offices in New York City, or e-mail staff@backinprint.com.

Printed in the United States
72862LV00004B/93-94